BUILDING A SECTIONAL LAYOUT

Pelle K. Søeborg

KB
KALMBACH BOOKS
WAUKESHA, WI

Kalmbach Books
21027 Crossroads Circle
Waukesha, Wisconsin 53186
www.KalmbachHobbyStore.com

Published in 2017
21 20 19 18 17   1 2 3 4 5

Manufactured in China

ISBN: 978-1-62700-380-3
EISBN: 978-1-62700-381-0

Photos: Pelle K. Søeborg
Layout and design: Pelle K. Søeborg (www.soeeborg.dk)
Editor: Randy Rehberg

Library of Congress Control Number: 2016943705

Contents

UP's Daneburg Subdivision:
a sectional layout with atmosphere

The American Midwest is characterized by wide open spaces and cornfields.

After three permanent layouts, I wanted my fourth, and most likely my last, layout to be movable. And I mean *movable* rather than portable. I have no intention of taking it to shows, but I wanted it to be easy to move, whether I ended up selling it or taking it (or sections of it) with me, when I one day move to a smaller place.

I designed a sectional system using standardized rectangular layout segments. The segments rest on a L-girder frame mounted on triangular gussets that attach to the walls at the studs. Without any legs resting on the floor, I gained a lot of free space under the layout. This gives the impression of having a wider aisle than it really is.

A layout starts with planning what you want your model railroad to do. The space I have available for a model railroad is very limited. My train room measures 11' x 22' which means I had to accept a lot of compromises when modeling in HO scale. You really have to prioritize your choices, as you can't have them all. Actually, you can only have a fragment of what you want. Instead of getting frustrated over all the things you can't do, you need to define your wishes for the layout you want to build and make a prioritized list. In many ways, layout planning and design is more about what can be left out rather than what can be included.

One problem with a sectional layout is that you have seams going through the scenery where the sections join. The seam is especially noticeable on roads and tracks.

There are advantages to building a small layout rather than a large one. One, you are able to finish it within a reasonable time period. It took me two-and-a-half years to build this one. Two, it costs less to build than a bigger layout. Three, it is easier to start over and build another layout if you get bored with the one you have.

Complex operation was not my main focus as I am the sole operator of my layout. My previous layout had some operation potential, but the only operation that actually took place was when I amused myself with a little switching at Daneville, the town on the layout, and at Duolith Cement, the largest industry on the layout, so my goal for operating possibilities on my new layout was limited to some switching. To be honest, I almost only run my trains if I have visitors coming to see my layout, so instead of focusing on operation, I wanted my layout to be interesting for visitors to look at. Basically, I just wanted a double-track main line, so I could run various trains for visitors and have one or two rail-served businesses to satisfy my modest personal needs for operation.

With my planning in place, I moved on to the layout's design. Designing a sectional layout is a little different from planning a permanent layout. On a permanent layout, you can customize the shape of your benchwork to fit a track plan. On a sectional layout, it is the other way around. The size of the layout sections defines the space for your track plan.

I wanted to model a Class I railroad set in the present time. My previous layout featured modern Union Pacific equipment, so I stayed with the UP. That way, I didn't have to buy new locomotives, which can become costly. I also wanted to model a main line so I would be able to run different types of trains. To capture the flavor of a main line, I need to run relatively long trains—with 30–35 cars, depending on the length of the cars. Modern trains require long staging tracks and broad curves, both of which take up

Private grade crossings are typical for rural areas where farmers need to cross the tracks to access their fields.

I needed good-looking trees for this scene with the farmhouse, and it took me several attempts to come up with a way to make the trees look realistic.

The Safety Kleen oil recycling business outside Daneburg is one of two rail-served businesses on my layout, and it can receive up to two tank cars at a time. My model is based on the Safety Kleen facility in Grand Island, Neb. Everything except the storage tanks are built from scratch.

space that I don't have, but I was willing to dedicate the needed space to have mainline running.

A good thing about building a sectional layout is that you can finish one section completely before moving on to the next. That way, you have a finished scene to look at sooner. On my previous layouts, which were all permanent ones, I finished one task completely before undertaking the next. After laying the track, I added all the basic terrain, then built the roads, including painting and weathering, and then constructed all the basic ground cover, etc., etc. … It took much longer before I had a finished scene.

However, there are some issues that are typical with a sectional layout. You can't avoid visible seams going through the scenery where the sections join. The seams are especially noticeable on roads and tracks. On areas with dirt, grass, and bushes, the seams are easier to camouflage so you can't tell where one

section ends and the next begins.

It is the same problem with the backdrop. Each layout segment has an associated backdrop section attached to it, and it leaves a vertical seam between the sections. Because my hidden staging runs

right behind the backdrop, the backdrop sections had to be free-standing and not mounted on the wall, so I couldn't make rounded corners, as on my previous layout. Using sharp corners, I did create a more eye-catching solution.

9

What makes a layout look realistic?

If you want to authentically model an actual prototype location in HO scale, you will soon find out that in a modestly sized layout room, your layout may have to be dramatically scaled down. A mile in HO scale is 60 feet long, and even a small rural town stretches over several miles, so scaling a real scene down without compressing it is just not possible in HO scale. In N or Z scales, you might have a better chance.

If you don't have room for modeling a specific place or area, do not despair. A fictitious place can look just as authentic. The easiest way to achieve good results is to base your fictitious place on various elements from real places. That way, you create a place that people can recognize and relate to.

When modeling a real location, or even a fictitious place, it is beneficial to visit the area you want to model. When I visit an area that I want to put on my layout, I don't just stay trackside. In the Midwest, I walked the streets of the small towns. I grabbed a bite at local diners and talked with the locals. I learned a lot about corn that way. In other words, focus on the big picture rather than on the details. Find what gives the area its atmosphere. I look for the common things rather than any spectacular things. In the actual modeling, I understate rather than overstate to make my point. If you overstate a scene too much, there is a risk that your layout will turn into a caricature.

I take pictures of many buildings that I may use as prototypes for the buildings on my layout. The buildings in the town on my layout are modeled after those in different towns and places, so even though the town on my layout is a fictitious place, several of the houses are models of actual buildings.

Your choice of colors plays an important role in achieving a realistic-looking layout. Pay attention to the colors

Every layout needs a signature structure—something people will remember that specific layout for. On my layout, the signature structure is a grain elevator complex, partly kitbashed and partly scratchbuilt. Based on one in Lexington, Neb., it is heavily compressed compared to the prototype, but it still dwarfs the trains enough to appear realistic.

If you model the Midwest, you need an old forgotten barn somewhere on the layout. I built this one from scratch.

of scenery in the real world. For example, a grass field might just look green, but if you take a closer look, you will notice that it has many shades of green, ranging from fresh green to beige and golden shades.

The same with concrete. It might appear a uniform gray at first glance, but it can contain gray, brown, and even black shades, depending on how old it is. This also applies to brickwork, asphalt, and wood.

The available space for a layout is often limited, so when you compose your scene, you have to be very selective. We have a tendency to incorporate more structures and other elements than space allows. That will not work if you want to create a realistic scene, and in most cases, some things may have to be eliminated. Spacing elements too closely together can spoil the illusion of a real place. You should also avoid adding distracting objects. This could be a structure that does not fit a location, such as putting a large fire station in a small-town block. It can also be a backdrop that doesn't match the colors of the layout. In other words, avoid anything that sticks out. That doesn't mean you can't have a signature structure that attracts attention, as do the grain silos on my layout. It just has to look as if it belongs in the scene.

One thing that will make a scene more interesting is not having your track and roads run parallel with the layout's edge. Instead, put them on a slight diagonal. And if you have a street running from the front edge to the back edge, don't put it at an exact 90-degree angle.

You don't need to apply a lot of details to a scene to create a desired effect. Sometimes, using just little things, such as a few signs and an old bathtub the farmer placed in the field as a drinking trough for his cows, adds a nice touch to a scene.

The Daneburg residential area is as typical as it can be with well-maintained two-story homes, green lawns, and shady trees.

As a mixed freight blasts through Daneburg, a UP signalman watches three railfans on the other side of the tracks.

The details you add to a scene can be the icing on the cake. While my layouts may appear very detailed, in fact, they are not. Realism is not directly proportional to the amount of detail you have in a scene. If a scene is cluttered with many small details, they may more or less neutralize each other for attention. It is much better to apply only a few details at select locations. This makes it easier for the viewer to spot them, and you can more easily control what you want a viewer to look at. Viewers will see the details but not notice any lack of details between that spot and the next—giving them the impression that your scene is very detailed.

My layouts have all been about creating impressions. I don't think I would be able to model a place that I haven't been to and breathed in its atmosphere. That is why I have never been tempted to model historic railroads. I don't think I would do a good job modeling something I have never seen with my own eyes.

Choice of location

"Why do you want to model the Midwest, with the most boring scenery in the U.S.?" I have been asked that question many times. The mostly flat Midwest may not be high on the list of many modelers, and that is actually one of the reasons I picked that specific area for my layout—instead of snow-capped peaks, rocky canyons, and forests of conifers. Not that I don't like those areas, but I have seen many well-executed examples of model railroads based on areas with spectacular scenery. The Heartland, however, you rarely see modeled.

I have traveled the Midwest several times, mainly in Iowa and Nebraska, and I like the area with its small rural towns and endless cornfields. The scenery might not be spectacular, but the American Midwest has its own magic, and that is exactly what I am trying to re-create—the atmosphere of a place, not necessarily

Although my layout features the relatively flat Midwest, you will find some hilly terrain on a part of the layout. It was my excuse to sneak a bridge in and solve the problem that the tracks had to cross over each other when entering and exiting the hidden staging.

spectacular scenery. In many ways, it can be more of a challenge to create an interesting model of flat, and at first glance, relatively uninteresting scenery than creating spectacular mountain scenery. The Midwest offered the modeling challenges I was looking for, and the UP runs right through there, so could I use the locomotives I had from my previous model railroad.

This book
This book is not meant as a detailed manual about building a layout from A to Z but to serve as an inspiration to you and help you make the right decisions when planning your next model railroad layout. I will show you examples of how to compose authentic-looking scenes and walk you through ways to execute them.

However, I do cover the basic topics such as benchwork construction and how to lay track. Even if you model a different area or time period, you can use many of my ideas and techniques on your layout.

Disclaimer
I try to create authentic-looking scenes, but that does not necessarily mean that

every detail is 100 percent prototypically correct. You can't be an expert in everything. I do research, but sometimes you just have to draw a line and get started on the project regardless if you don't have all the information you need to be sure if what you are making is prototypically correct. If I had to research every little detail that I am adding to my layout, I would spend more time researching than on building a layout—and that is not my priority. My definition of success is that a scene should make someone feel like they have been there, a place they can relate to. It doesn't bother me if a telephone pole is placed a foot too close to the road or if an air conditioner is the wrong type for the area I am modeling. Believe me, I get a lot of comments from people who are experts in specific fields who spot these kinds of flaws on my layout. Of course, they only mean well, and I have received useful information that way, but often I don't bother correcting my wrongs as long as they are not crucial errors. Call it poetic license.

This is the view that visitors see when they enter my train room.

The layout at a glance

The layout is sectional and consists of five straight sections, four corner sections, and two custom-designed sections at the entrance. The track plan is a simple double oval with hidden staging behind the backdrop.

The layout's wiring is sectional too. All the wiring between the layout sections is connected by 25-pin connectors, except for the buzz wires, which are connected via screw terminals.

All the turnouts are controlled via a single control panel attached to the fascia on the center layout section. Next to the control panel, you will find two connector panels for my Lenz DCC control system.

Monitoring the hidden staging is done via a vehicle backup camera kit that I bought in an auto supply store. It was the simplest and cheapest solution I could find.

As I often have several visitors at the same time, I made the aisle as wide as possible, so two people can pass each other comfortably.

Framing the layout

Using a valance and fascia to frame the scenes makes for a better presentation. I added a fascia consisting of ¼" MDF board to the front of each layout section. I attached a corresponding valance to the ceiling.

I painted my valance and fascia dark gray. In my opinion, a dark contrasting color frames and highlights the modeled scenes better than if the valance and fascia are painted in a color that matches the scenery.

The lighting on the layout consists of full-spectrum 4000° Kelvin fluorescent light tubes mounted behind the valance.

Removable items

I wanted as many things as possible to be easy to remove if I later wanted to reuse them on another layout or just wanted them out of the way while I was working on that part of the layout, so I did not glue down many items on this layout.

The lighting on the layout consists of full-spectrum 4000° Kelvin fluorescent light tubes mounted on the ceiling right behind the valance. I painted the back side of the valance white so it would reflect the light better.

When you enter my layout room, you have to pass through two simple gates. My first idea was to make a lift-out section with scenery so it could be a part of the layout. I built the section from plywood, but it became obvious that it was too heavy and difficult to handle, so I scrapped it and made the gates instead.

All operations of the layout take place via a turnout control panel and two Lenz connector panels mounted on the fascia on the layout's center section. Via a small monitor on the valance, I can monitor the hidden staging.

The gates swing up and attach to the valance with magnets.

Each gate is attached to the benchwork with a small hinge. To power the tracks on the gates, I soldered a small feeder wire between the gap between the rails.

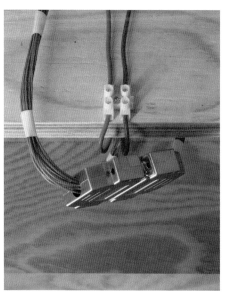

25-pin connectors connect all the wiring between the layout sections except for the buzz wires, which are connected via screw terminals.

I made a socket system for the signals on my layout, so they can easily be pulled out if needed.

I mounted fold-out cup holders on the fascia. Besides serving their intended purpose, they turned out to be very useful as tool holders as well.

The signals on my layout are an example of that. I invented a mounting system for them, so I could just plug them in and pull them up without using any glue to hold them. Basically, I made a socket for each signal and extended the four legs on the signal post with pieces of styrene tube. The socket is attached to the layout, and then I just plug the signal bridge into it. It is a tight fit, so the signal is stable but can easily be pulled out if needed.

Many of the structures are also not glued to the layout.

Of course, some pieces had to be glued down, and on those, I used ordinary white carpenter's glue, which can be dissolved with water.

Remaining issues

There are still a few things on the layout that I haven't found a solution for. among

At each end of the layout, I mounted a shelf, where I can conveniently unpack trains or perform maintenance and minor repairs.

them is a control system for the signals. As my layout is meant for show rather than operation, I will probably settle for a photocell-based system like the one that operates my grade crossing.

Custom-made control panel

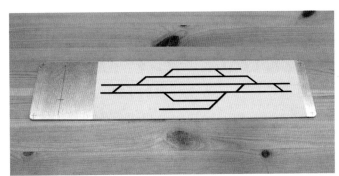

1. I made the control panel from a .080" (2mm) sheet of aluminum cut to the correct size. I printed out a schematic drawing of the track arrangement that I had made on my computer and glued it to the aluminum sheet using 3M repositionable spray mount. Using the print as a template, I drilled the holes for the toggle switches.

2. After the holes were drilled, I removed the print and cleaned the glue from the surface of the aluminum with thinner. I spray-painted the panel flat black and let it dry before I re-created the track arrangement with masking tape, using the holes for the toggle switches as guides.

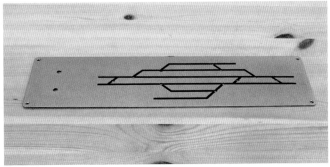

3. I then spray-painted the panel silver so it matched my Lenz DCC connector panels. After removing the masking tape, I coated the panel with a satin finish.

4. I installed the toggle switches in the pre-drilled holes on the panel. I soldered wires to the toggle switches and collected all the wires in a 25-pin plug.

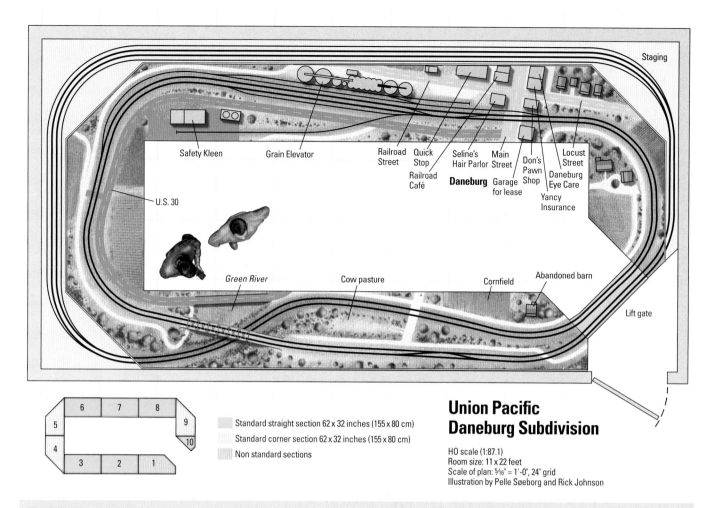

Safety Kleen   Grain Elevator

Railroad Street   Quick Stop

Railroad Café

Seline's Hair Parlor   Main Street

Daneburg   Garage for lease

Don's Pawn Shop

Yancy Insurance

Locust Street   Daneburg Eye Care

U.S. 30

Green River   Cow pasture   Cornfield   Abandoned barn

Staging

Lift gate

Standard straight section 62 x 32 inches (155 x 80 cm)
Standard corner section 62 x 32 inches (155 x 80 cm)
Non standard sections

Union Pacific Daneburg Subdivision

HO scale (1:87.1)
Room size: 11 x 22 feet
Scale of plan: 5/16" = 1'-0", 24" grid
Illustration by Pelle Søeborg and Rick Johnson

The layout at a glance

Name: Union Pacific Daneburg Subdivision

Scale: HO

Size: 11 x 22 feet (3.3 x 6.6 meters)

Prototype: UP

Locale: Freelanced U.S. Midwest, inspired by eastern Nebraska and western Iowa

Era: Present

Layout style: Walk-in

Mainline run: 60 feet (excluding staging)

Minimum radius: 33"

Track: Flextrack, code 83 on main line, code 70 on sidings, and code 55 on spurs

Turnouts: No 6

Maximum grade: 1 percent

Height: 46" to 50" (115 to 125 cm)

Scenery: Foam insulation board

Backdrop: Photographic

Control: Lenz DCC

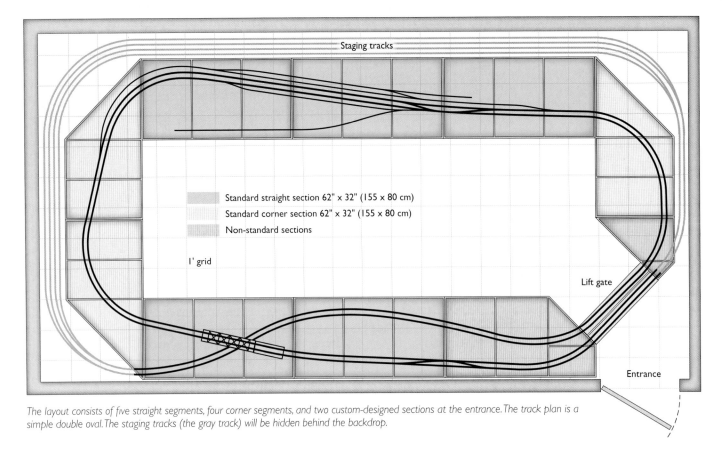

Staging tracks

Standard straight section 62" x 32" (155 x 80 cm)
Standard corner section 62" x 32" (155 x 80 cm)
Non-standard sections

1' grid

Lift gate

Entrance

The layout consists of five straight segments, four corner segments, and two custom-designed sections at the entrance. The track plan is a simple double oval. The staging tracks (the gray track) will be hidden behind the backdrop.

It all starts with the benchwork

One lesson I learned from cutting up my Daneville layout in sections was that no matter how careful you are, you can't do it without doing some damage to the track and scenery. So after three permanent layouts, this time I wanted to build a sectional layout. I wanted it to be movable rather than portable. I didn't have any intentions of taking it to shows and such, but I wanted it to be easy to move if I ended up selling it, or if I move to another place and have room for it.

I designed a sectional system using standardized rectangular layout segments. The segments rest on an L-girder frame mounted on triangular gussets that attach to the walls at the studs. Without any legs resting on the floor, I gained a lot of free space under the layout which makes the aisle look bigger than it really is.

I used 1 x 2s for most of the framework. Only the braces were made from 2 x 2s. I assembled the framework with screws only. I didn't use any glue because it will be easier to dismantle the framework later. When you don't use

glue in the assembly process, you have to be very precise when cutting the lumber.

I am definitely not a good carpenter, and my previous layout benchwork has been far from perfect. The key to making benchwork better is in the tools you use. I invested in a circular saw with adjustable cutting angles, and it made a world of difference when cutting lumber for the benchwork. For the first time

The old layout is gone, and before starting on the new one, I fixed up the room a bit. As my new layout is different in size and shape from the old one, I also moved the light fixtures in the ceiling, so they would fit the new layout. It is much easier to do this without the layout in your way. You can place a stepladder exactly where you want to when you are working.

in my life, I was able to make perfectly straight cuts.

The size of the layout sections was defined by the size of my train room. Each section measured 62" x 32". The layout sections were made from ½" plywood screwed and glued together. I used MDF board for my previous layout, which is more sound-deadening than plywood, but it is also quite a bit heavier. Keeping the weight of the sections down was a high priority, so I went with plywood for this layout. The benchwork sections supporting the town and grain elevator scene were entirely covered with sheets of plywood. For sections having more hilly terrain, I made the subroadbed of plywood, with the surrounding landscape made of foam insulation board.

The staging tracks run along the walls and will be hidden behind the layout's backdrop. I discovered that one benefit of building a sectional layout is that I could remove the layout sections in front of the staging areas and gain full access to these areas while I was working on them.

Each gusset consists of three pieces of wood. I first attached 1 x 2s to the wall. I then fastened a horizontal 1 x 2 to it. I attached a temporary support leg to the other end. I then clamped a 2 x 2 diagonal support beam to the vertical 1 x 2 and screwed it to the 1 x 2 on the wall first and then to the horizontal 1 x 2.

I designed a sectional system using standardized rectangular layout segments. I made them from ½" plywood. Each segment consisted of two longitudinal and four transverse plywood sheets. I assembled each layout segment with both screws and glue.

I made shelves for storage under the layout. It is easier to keep the room clean if you don't have too much stuff on the floor.

To make benchwork stable when assembled with only screws places a high demand on exact sawing. A 45-degree cut has to be exactly 45 degrees. The slightest deviation will create both visible and construction problems.

I made two types of layout segments: a rectangular type for regular sections and another for corner sections. The holes in the transverse plywood sheets are for the wiring.

The layout segments are attached to each other with two bolts and wing nuts. If you need to remove a section, you just have to loosen the bolts in each end and pull the segment out.

I attached an L-girder frame to the triangular gussets. Again, I used 1 x 2s, but if you have a larger span between the supports than I do, you might want to use 1 x 3s or larger supports. The shelf against the wall is for the staging which will be hidden behind the backdrop.

Here, the layout segments are placed on the framework. Note that I made the segments in two heights. The ones on the left are for the flat town area, and they are covered with plywood sheets. The ones on the right are lower and have an open frame for a more hilly terrain. Yours truly is studying the track plan and preparing for the next move.

Subroadbed

On half of the layout segments, the scenery will be completely flat, so they were covered with plywood sheets that will serve both as the subroadbed and subterrain. On the remaining layout segments, the terrain will be more hilly and the subroadbed sections were cut from ½" plywood and attached to each layout segment on risers.

Because the track crosses over itself, I couldn't totally avoid grades. Since the layout features flatter terrain, I was able to keep them below 1 percent.

To access my previous layouts, you had to pass under a duckunder, which turned out to be very impractical because of the number of visitors I had, so I wanted to avoid that on this layout. My first idea was to make a lift-out section with scenery, so it could be a part of the layout. I built the section from plywood, but even before I added the scenery, it became obvious that it was too heavy and difficult to handle, so I scrapped the idea and solved the problem with gates instead. The gates swing up and attach to the valance with magnets.

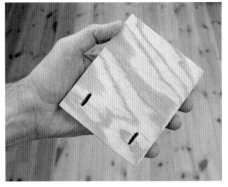

Because the track crosses over itself, my layout will have an approximately 1 percent grade. Grades can be difficult to establish with 100 percent precision, so I made adjustable risers for the subroadbed. That way, I could adjust the grade after the subroadbed was in place.

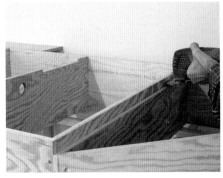

The track had to enter a gentle grade on the layout segments at each end of the flat town area, so I cut a notch in the transverse plywood sheets below the track.

Before cutting the pieces for the subroadbed, I made a cardboard mock-up of the route.

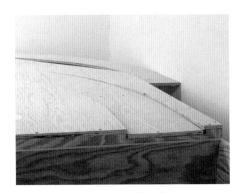

I then made a cut on each side of the subroadbed and let it flex down. I wanted to be able to adjust the height later, if necessary, so I only attached it with a screw—no glue.

I placed the cardboard pieces on the remaining plywood sheets, trying to figure out how to best utilize them.

I outlined the cardboard templates on the plywood with a pencil and cut out the subroadbed pieces with a jigsaw.

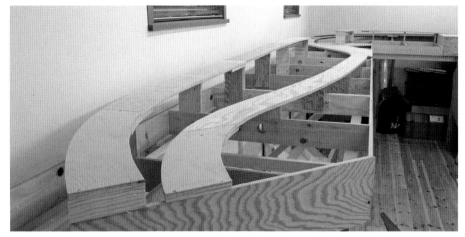

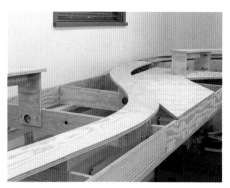

I didn't yet know how long my bridge would be exactly, so the gap is a little wider than the bridge was.

A view of the finished subroadbed shows how the upper track will cross over the lower track. Both the upper track and the lower track have a grade to gain enough clearance for a double-stack car to pass under the bridge.

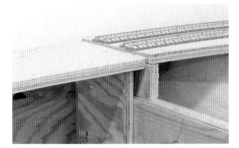

Adjustable risers will also make it easier to adjust the individual height between the subroadbed where the staging track enters the layout because mainline track and staging track will rest on different thicknesses of cork.

Sometimes it turns out that your ingenious design is not nearly as brilliant as you thought. A riser had to be placed exactly where one of the bolts that holds the layout segments together and where the hole for the wiring is. I solved the problem by cutting a corresponding hole in the riser.

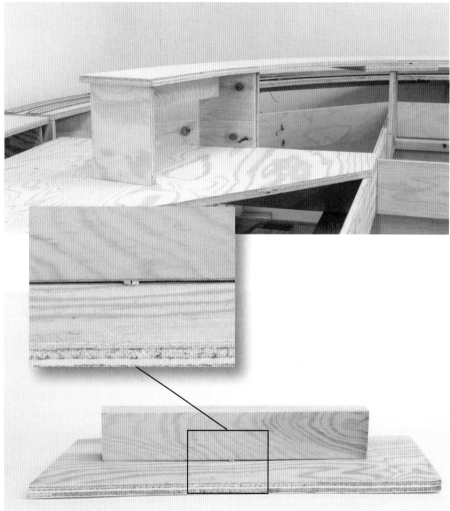

Building a sectional layout sometimes has challenges you wouldn't have on a permanent layout. The track leading to a bridge had a grade, and usually I would just let the subroadbed gradually flex to level on the last 12"–15" before the bridge, but unfortunately, the last 12" of subroadbed before the bridge was placed on a new layout section and, therefore, not attached to the subroadbed with the grade, which is on another section. To avoid a kink where the two sections of subroadbed joined, I placed a block of wood on the underside of the plywood roadbed and placed a small piece of stripwood between the wood block and the plywood. I screwed the roadbed to the wood block at each end, forcing it to create a slightly arched shape that matched a gentle transition from a 1 percent grade to level.

You don't find much straight track on my layout. Track that could just as well have been totally straight is slightly curved. Fluid trackwork like this is so much more interesting to look at than straight track with curves at only each corner of the room.

Laying the track

Laying track is one of my absolute favorite tasks in the process of building a model railroad. It is very tranquilizing work. It doesn't require great mental effort to lay track, and one's thoughts can wander unhindered. It is also work you can leave and easily come back to. It doesn't need any planning or preparation, and it is not messy, so you don't need to clean any tools when you stop. The tools you need for laying track are a rail cutter—I use a rotary tool with a cutting disc—a soldering iron, a sharp hobby knife for trimming ties, and a drill for making holes in the roadbed for feeder wires.

I model the present time, so most of my mainline track has concrete ties except in the turnouts and a short stretch of the main line that represents track that has not yet been upgraded.

There are no turnouts with concrete ties available in HO scale, so I had no choice but to use turnouts with wood ties. Fortunately, it is quite prototypical to use turnouts with wood ties together with track with concrete ties. I have seen turnouts with concrete ties on the UP main line between Chicago and North Platte, Neb., but the most common practice on U.S. railroads still seems to be using wood ties on turnouts. I have been told that it is because the total cost of a turnout with concrete ties is much higher.

Another big factor is that, if a train derails and starts pounding ties for a few miles, almost every concrete tie will need to be replaced before the line can be reopened due to broken ties. Concrete can't flex, and it will break and crack. If the same thing happened with wood ties, there would be a really good chance that many of the wood ties could be left in place for removal at a later time, allowing the line to be reopened sooner without the loss of revenue on that line.

If they are not damaged in derailments, concrete ties last longer than wood ties. Because of their weight, concrete ties are better than wood ties at keeping welded rail from developing sun kinks in heavily curved mainline track.

I have used commercially made flextrack and turnouts on all my layouts, and I didn't see any reason to deviate from that plan on this layout. I have been tempted to give handlaid track with real wood ties a try, but I actually think that flextrack looks more realistic.

Before I started laying track on the actual layout, I applied cork and laid Peco code 83 track for the hidden staging, which is an exception from the rest of the layout's track.

Applying the roadbed

On my previous layout, I applied a ¼"-thick layer of a sound-deadening material between the plywood and the cork roadbed. The sound-deadening sheets are very heavy, and I didn't apply them to this layout because I wanted to keep the weight of the sections as low as possible. Instead, I used two layers of cork. The first layer is .080" (2mm) high. The height of the second layer depends on the type of the track. For mainline track, I used 0.2" (5mm) cork, and for secondary track, I used .080" (2mm) cork.

The width of the .080" base layer exceeds both sides of the track roadbed, so the ballast will rest on cork instead of on plywood. I thought that, as long as the ballast, which will turn hard as glass when it is glued with thinned white glue, rested on something soft and flexible, instead of directly on plywood, it would somewhat minimize the wheel noise. It did help but was not as effective as the sound-deadening layer on my previous layout.

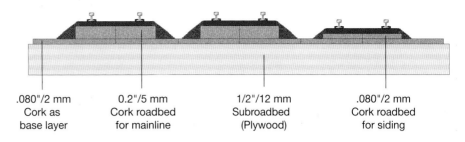

.080"/2 mm Cork as base layer	0.2"/5 mm Cork roadbed for mainline	1/2"/12 mm Subroadbed (Plywood)	.080"/2 mm Cork roadbed for siding

To make it easier to draw curves with easements, I made a curve-with-easement ruler. The inner edge of the ruler is for the inner curve, and the outer edge is for the outer curve. The minimum curve radius on my layout is 33".

I also made turnout templates so I could establish the exact position of the turnouts. I made the templates by taking a photo of a turnout and then printing out a couple of copies on my printer at 1:1 scale. I glued the prints to sheets of cardboard and then cut them out.

The cork roadbed I intended to use for the mainline track was so thick that the spikes holding the track would not reach the plywood. I therefore glued small wood blocks under the track where the layout sections joined, so I could fasten the track ends on each section properly.

I bought cork in large rolls and cut my own roadbed. It is probably cheaper than buying commercial cork roadbed, but that is not the main reason. I did it because I can customize the width of the strips. I used a temporary work table that I made from lumber left over from the benchwork. I cut the cork strips with a sharp hobby knife using a steel ruler as a guide.

For gluing cork to the plywood, and cork to cork, I used a sealant glue that stays flexible. You typically use this type of glue between the planks on a boat deck.

I laid strips of cork for the base layer along the centerlines for the track. That way I could still trace the track's center after it had been covered with cork.

To even out the glue underneath the cork, I rolled a rolling pin over the cork a couple of times.

I kept adding strip after strip along the track centerlines until the area was completely covered with a base layer of cork.

In curves and other places where the cork wasn't laid in straight lines, I held the strips in place with push pins until the glue had dried.

I used two thicknesses of cork for the track roadbed: 0.2" for mainline track and .080" for sidings. I cut strips in half width-wise and laid the strips along the joint between the base layer strips that followed the track centerline.

The transition between the thick 0.2" and the thin .080" roadbed was completed in steps. The first step down was made of two layers of .080" cork, and the second of .120" cork strips.

I sanded the transition steps smooth with a power sander.

I covered the small wood blocks placed where the layout sections join with a thin layer of cork.

Laying the track

I use three different rail sizes on my layout. For all mainline track, I use code 83, and for secondary track and sidings, I use code 70. Then I have a single spur on which I use code 55. I soldered the joints on the track on each layout section and left small gaps between the rails for expansion where the layout sections join. To ensure reliable operation on my layout, I soldered feeder wires to every track section.

I don't glue my track to the roadbed but attach it only with spikes. It is a quick method for mounting track, and it allows you to easily adjust a section of track simply by pulling up a couple of spikes and readjusting it.

Laying track on a sectional layout offers the challenge that the rail has to be cut exactly where each section ends. At these joints, I didn't use rail joiners but just butted the track sections up against each other. If this happens in the middle of a curve, it can be a bit tricky—but not impossible. You just need to fasten the rail as close to the edge as possible with spikes to keep it in place.

Laying perfectly straight track is not easy to do. The best way to check if track is straight is to look down the track from the lowest possible angle. You will then see even the slightest kink. Still it is not easy to lay it completely straight. Real railroads seem to have the same problem. If you look down almost any type of track, it will have kinks and dips. Some secondary track even looks so uneven that you

may wonder how a train can stay on it. With the comforting knowledge that not having completely straight track is very prototypical, I began laying the track.

I prefer laying the more complicated track sections, such as a crossover, first and then working my way out from there.

There is actually not much straight track on my layout. Of course, there are the unavoidable curves defined by the size of the layout room, but I also have slightly curved track that just as well could have been totally straight. Fluid trackwork is so much more interesting to look at than straight track that turns into a curve only at the corners of the room.

I like the look of superelevated curves and wanted to have some on this layout too. Superelevated curves do not improve how trains operate on the track. On

the contrary, they can cause problems with tall cars tilting too much or causing derailments, especially on long trains. With my new layout being a sectional one, superelevated curves could be more of a problem. Anyway, I wanted to give it a try. I superelevated the curves by pushing bits of styrene under the outer ties. I started with .010", then .020" and .030", and ended with .040" at max elevation. The transition from base level to max elevation takes place over a distance of 12"–15". I didn't glue the styrene bits. That way, I could easily remove them again if the superelevation turned out to cause any problems for the trains. I thoroughly tested different types of trains before ballasting the track.

I have always liked Micro Engineering's track and have used their track for my two

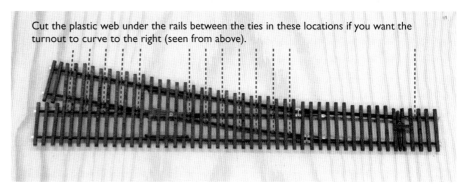

Cut the plastic web under the rails between the ties in these locations if you want the turnout to curve to the right (seen from above).

Start with the more complicated trackwork such as a crossover. I placed the crossover where the main line curves slightly, far more gentle than any curved turnout would be, so I modified two Micro Engineering No. 6 turnouts to fit the curve. I cut the plastic web under the rails in numerous places except on one side, so I could shape the turnout to fit the curve.

Cut the ties on each turnout so they fit the distance between the two mainline tracks. Remove a frog rail on each turnout. Be careful not to damage the little tabs that hold the rail when you pull it out. Leave the stock rail intact.

Push the turnouts together. The bare stock rail on each turnout will slide in where the removed frog rails were. Again, be very careful not to damage the little tabs that hold the rails as you do so.

previous layouts, and I had no intention to change that on this layout. All the turnouts and flextrack with wood ties on my layout are from Micro Engineering, and I planned to use ME track for the track with concrete ties also, but it was unavailable when I was ready to start laying track, so I ordered some Walthers track instead. Then after I had laid all the Walthers track with concrete ties and had most of it painted and weathered, a package with ME flextrack with concrete ties surprisingly showed up. I had forgotten to cancel my original ME order before I ordered the Walthers track. I was caught in a dilemma. The easy solution was to ignore the fact that I gotten the ME track and keep the Walthers track, or I could rip out all the newly laid Walthers track and replace it with the better looking ME track. I took a deep breath and replaced the Walthers

track with the ME track. I normally try to avoid doing the same work twice, but I just knew it would always nag at me if I had kept the Walthers track on my layout.

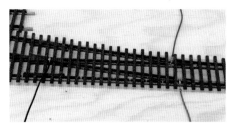

Before I spiked the turnouts in place, I soldered feeder wires to the closure rails and the frog. The power on the points rely on electrical contact between the point and the stock rail. A more reliable solution is soldering feeder wires to the points. The frog on Micro Engineering turnouts is insulated and the power to it has to change polarity, depending on how the turnout is set. That is easily done if you use Tortoise switch machines as I do. Each machine has two sets of contacts that you can wire your frog to for power routing.

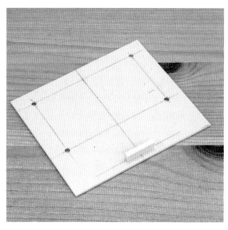

I made a template for attaching the Tortoise switch machines. It consisted of a sheet of .040" styrene with four holes for the screws. The tab marks the position of the slot for the throw-bar pin. I placed the template under the roadbed with the tab in the slot and drilled the four holes for the screws.

One more thing needed to be done before the turnouts could be put in place—making a slot in the roadbed for the throw-bar pin. I started by cutting a slot in the cork where I had marked the position of the throw bar.

Then I drilled through the plywood. I made three holes next to each other, used a milling head to remove the wood between the holes, and ended up with a ½"-wide slot.

I spiked the crossover to the roadbed. Because of the cuts I made in the plastic web under the rails, the turnouts easily fit the gentle curve that the main line makes at that spot.

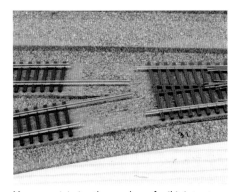

You can minimize the number of rail joints at turnouts by replacing the frog rails with rail from the adjacent flextrack. This can, of course, only be done if the rail is the same size. Where code 70 meets code 83, you have to keep the frog rail as it is.

Push the bare rail on each piece of flextrack in between the little tabs that held the removed frog rails.

The frogs on ME turnouts are insulated by a little gap between the adjacent rails and the frog. I filled these gaps with brown styrene glued with cyanoacrylate adhesive (CA). When the glue was dry, I trimmed the styrene bits with a scalpel so they followed the shape of the rail. This operation is purely for cosmetic reasons.

I didn't glue my flextrack but only attached it with spikes. Push the spikes in the roadbed at an angle when you attach your flextrack to a soft material like cork. It holds the rail better than if you push the spikes down vertically.

The track on each layout section is cut exactly where the section ends. The track continues on the adjacent section, but it is not connected with rail joiners. I leave a little gap between the rails to compensate for expansion.

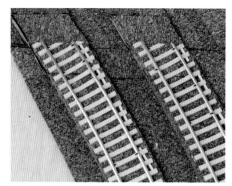

It becomes a little more tricky when two sections join in a curve. When flextrack is cut diagonally in the middle of a curve like this, it is not easy to align the rails between two sections. I spiked the rail ends as close to the edge as possible to keep them in place.

I use different sizes of rail on my layout depending on the type of track it represents. For mainline track I use code 83 rail, for sidings I use code 70 rail, and for spurs I use code 55 rail. Spurs often have wider-spaced ties than track that handles more traffic, so I cut the web between the ties on this Micro Engineering flextrack and spaced out the ties more.

The joints between the different sizes of rail were connected using the classic solution of squeezing a rail joiner flat in the end where the smallest rail connects and soldering the rail to it.

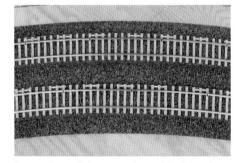

I superelevated the curves by pushing bits of styrene under the ties. I started with .010", then .020" and .030", and ended with .040" at max elevation. The transition from the base level to max elevation takes place over a distance of 12"–15". I didn't glue the styrene bits in case I needed to remove or adjust anything.

Here, you can see track applied to two straight layout sections and one corner section. The staging tracks to the left will be hidden behind the backdrop.

Painting the track

The key to having realistic-looking track is to paint it. I don't go crazy with painting ties in all kinds of different shades, although I have seen excellent examples of that. You can achieve good-looking results with less. My method of painting track consists of several steps. I first airbrush the track with a base color: light gray for track with wood ties, and a custom-mixed concrete color for track with concrete ties. Then I give the wood ties a black-brown wash. The rail, including the rail clips on track with concrete ties, is brush-painted in a gray-brown color mixed from ModelMaster Earth Gray and Sand. Finally, I weather the concrete track along the rails with brown powdered chalk.

I normally paint my track after it has been applied to the layout and did so with most of the track on this layout too. The only exception was the ME track that replaced the Walthers track. To avoid getting paint on the finished track with wood ties that was already in place, I airbrushed the sections of ME flextrack with concrete ties before I installed them. Only the rail was painted after the installation because it was done by hand with a brush.

Before airbrushing the track, you need to mask places where you don't want paint, such as between the switch point and stock rail on turnouts so it won't interfere with the electrical contact. To mask, I slipped small pieces of foam insulation board between the parts.

First, I airbrushed the track with wood ties a light gray color.

Paint dust is an unavoidable part of airbrushing, so to suck up the most of the dust, I placed the hose of a vacuum cleaner close to the area I was working on and turned it on while I used the airbrush. Dust particles can float around in the room for quite a while, so I left the vacuum cleaner on for about 10 minutes after I stopped using the airbrush to get most of paint dust.

Track with concrete ties received a custom-mixed concrete color mixed from equal amounts of Model Master 1730 Flat Gull Gray, 1706 Sand, and 1768 Flat White.

I scraped the paint off the top of the rails with a chisel blade. If you paint the rails and wood ties right after they have received the base color, you can wait with removing the paint from the top of the rails until the paint job has been completed. If you don't paint the rest right away, it will be best not to let the paint harden too much before you remove it.

I stained the wood ties with a mix of equal amounts of Vallejo 042 Cam Black Brown and 055 Gray Green with some Vallejo 061 Airbrush Thinner added to the mix.

I brush-painted all the rail with a grimy grayish-brown color mixed from ModelMaster Earth Gray and Sand in a 2:1 ratio.

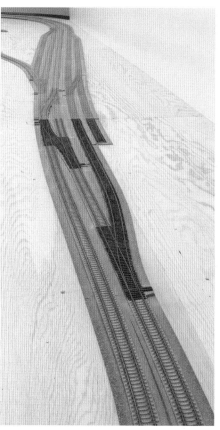

On track with concrete ties, I also painted the rail and rail clips with the ModelMaster Earth Gray and Sand mix.

To finish, I weathered the concrete track along the rails with brown powdered chalk.

Here, the painting and weathering of the track on the first layout section is completed. The track on the next two sections has only received the base color.

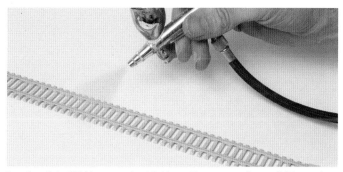

I replaced the Walthers track with Micro Engineering flextrack. To avoid getting paint on the track already in place, I airbrushed the pieces of flextrack concrete gray before I installed them.

I also painted the rail clips before installing the track. It was easier to do this on my workbench. I didn't want to paint the rail until the track had been installed because the track will be shaped to fit curves, and it will leave little shiny spots of bare metal on the rails if it had been painted in advance.

I replaced the Walthers track piece by piece with ME track.

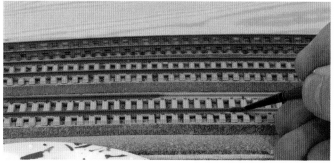

I painted the rails on the new track. Then I weathered it with powdered chalks the same as I did with the Walthers track.

A well-made backdrop that blends together with the scenery will expand your layout by many miles.

Adding a photo backdrop

The purpose of a backdrop is to give the illusion that our layout exceeds its actual physical space—to give the feeling of distance. And it doesn't take much to create that illusion. Actually you can get a long way with just a blue sky, but having some amount of distant scenery will provide an even better result.

Keep in mind that the focus should still be on your trains and modeled scenery. You don't want the backdrop to be the first thing that catches a viewer's eye when

entering the train room, so try to avoid spectacular landscapes and distracting elements. You also have to pay attention to color choice. If you prefer to paint your backdrop, then avoid bright colors. Distance mutes tones.

You no longer need to be a skilled artist to get a nice-looking backdrop. The digital revolution has made it easy for us who are not Rembrandts to create realistic-looking backdrops for our layouts. All you need is a digital camera and

photo-editing software. The first step is to go and shoot photos for your backdrop. It is not possible to have just one picture cover an entire backdrop unless you only need a short section of backdrop for a diorama. You will have to piece a backdrop together with several pictures. On a trip to Iowa and Nebraska, the locale of my layout, I took a whole bunch of photos of distant scenery, so I had something to work with for my backdrop. I also took pictures of small-town Main Streets to

extend a town scene on my layout. As I had no clue how this would work on my backdrop, I took these pictures from various perspectives and used telephoto and wide angle lenses.

Keep the horizon on your backdrop low. How low depends upon whether you primarily want it for visitors to see or for a background when taking photos of your layout from a low angle. On my previous layout, I designed the backdrop to be optimal for viewing, and when I took

pictures of the layout, the horizon looked too high. On this layout, I decided on a lower horizon. It looks perfect on pictures, and a little low when you stand and look at the layout. The rule of thumb is that you don't want a horizon higher than 3" or 4", even if the backdrop is designed for viewing. On this backdrop, the horizon is only 1"–1.5" high, which gives the illusion of a great distance in photos.

Be aware that when the photos you take for your backdrop are blown up to

backdrop size, the objects closest to the camera will probably be out of scale. For this reason, I only used the backgrounds of the photos.

I make minor color adjustments on the individual images so they match, but I don't make any general color adjustments before I have put the entire backdrop image together. Make sure to have a test print made before you have the entire backdrop printed out. The colors might look fine on your computer screen but they may turn out differently when printed.

Also, the type of light in your layout room influences how the colors will look. Placing a test print where the backdrop will be reveals if the colors need to be adjusted, and trust me, they do. Quite a bit actually. This is the second photographic backdrop I've created, so I knew my photos needed to have the colors adjusted. As a graphic designer, I am used to preparing photos for print, but I still needed to have several test prints made before I was pleased with the colors on my backdrop.

I had my backdrop printed out at a professional print shop. I prepared a series of lightweight PVC boards that matched the size of the layout sections on which the printer could mount the prints on. I could have done it myself and saved some money, but a professional printer will definitely do a better job, so why bother with it.

If you intend to keep your backdrop for a long time, I suggest that you have it coated with a UV protective film. If you don't, it will eventually fade. Also, if you have it printed on glossy paper and coat it with a flat film, the print will appear crisper and have better contrast.

Before I had the entire backdrop printed out, I had a test print made to see how it looked under the layout's lighting. The one at the right was the first printout. It turned out too red and dark, so I adjusted the colors on the photo file. The second test print turned out fine. The little test print between the two big prints is a print of the backdrop behind the town scene.

The backdrop prints were applied to lightweight PVC boards. You can get these boards in various thicknesses. I chose 0.4" (10mm) boards because they are rigid enough to stand alone without any support which was required because my staging is just behind the backdrop so I couldn't mount the boards on the wall. As my layout is in sections, the backdrop was made in sections at the same length as the layout sections. I glued pieces of PVC to the backs of the boards to create an interlocking system so the boards are flush at the joints when you push them together.

The top picture is one of the original photos I took in Iowa for the backdrop. The one below is the same photo after it was cropped and color adjusted to match the scenery materials I use and the layout's lighting. As you can see, I only used the top half of the original image. Objects close to the camera will appear out of scale on a backdrop so use only background objects. The colors needed quite a bit of adjustment. The layout's light is much weaker than real sunlight, so if you use the picture as is, it will appear too dark and lack contrast.

To avoid reflections from the light fixtures, I had the prints coated with a flat film, which also protects the prints from UV light. As you can see, I have sharp corners on my backdrop which are more noticeable than rounded corners. This is due to the 0.4" boards I used. They can't flex. If you want round corners, you have to use PVC boards 0.15" or thinner.

Putting the pieces together

Although I took more than 50 pictures of Midwestern scenery for my backdrop, I ended up using only 3 of them plus a sky image extracted from one of the photos. The area the backdrop will cover on the layout is three times wider than the section shown below but I simply repeated the image, so you, in principle, can make the backdrop as wide as you like.

The first layer is the sky. I used the sky from one of my scenery photos. The sky was not wide enough to fit the width of the entire backdrop, so I stretched it using the scale tool. I also stretched it vertically as I also needed a taller sky. Had there been clouds in my sky picture, it would not have been possible to stretch it because the clouds would be distorted. Instead, I would have had to use numerous sky images or add the clouds later to the wide blue sky.

Next came the landscape. I picked one of my many landscape photos and removed the sky from it and placed it on the next layer. I scaled it to HO scale. You don't want any object in the foreground like a fence or a pole to be bigger than 1:87. Objects can be smaller, as they will just look like they are farther away.

I picked another of my landscape photos, removed the sky, and placed it on the third layer. My landscape pictures were taken at different times of the day and even on different days, so the lighting was never the same. I adjusted the color of the field in this layer, so it matched the color on the landscape on the second layer. With Adobe Photoshop, this can be done in various ways. I used the curves.

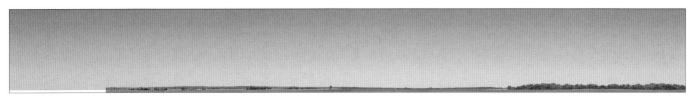

In the new layer, I expanded the scenery with another of my landscape photos. As on the previous two, I removed the sky and adjusted the color. Where the landscape sections join, I let them overlap a little and softened the edge to blend the seams together by adding a layer mask and painting a soft mask with the airbrush tool.

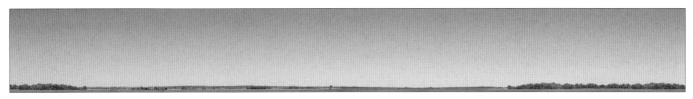

For the last landscape section, I used the same image as the first but reversed it. I kept a very low horizon on this backdrop. A low horizon looks great when you photograph your layout from a low angle. A higher horizon is a better option when standing and viewing your layout. You have to decide whether your backdrop should be designed for photography or viewing, and place the horizon accordingly.

Creating a rural scene

Making scenery is probably the most rewarding phase in building a layout. This is when you turn your model railroad into a place people relate to, whether you model a specific location or a totally fictional place. I am not modeling a specific place but am trying to recreate the flavor of eastern Nebraska and western Iowa. The scene is relatively flat with only minor height differences and, in contrast to my previous layouts, very green.

Making green scenery was new to me, and working with flock grass required a little practice, both applying it and blending realistic-looking shades. Fortunately, there are many great-looking scenery materials available nowadays.

I dedicated the two corner sections at one end of the layout to being modeled as typical Midwest farmland. There is no doubt that a scene like this is better suited for featuring straight track sections, so I didn't have any high hopes that it

would be possible to create a convincing Midwest farmland scene here. You don't see many areas in the Midwest where the track and roads are not straight as an arrow, and the track here is one big curve and the road curves too. However, the result turned out better than I expected.

The first step is choosing the elements you want to model in the scene. In addition to the tracks, the key elements in a farmland scene are the fields. Typical crops for the Midwest are corn and soybeans. When it comes to HO scale cornstalks, you can choose from several brands. I chose cornstalks from Busch. It took a lot of

packages, and money, to cover the cornfields on this scene. To my knowledge, no soybean crops are offered, so I had to custom-make them, but it turned out to be quite easy and cheaper to make than the corn.

Another typical scenic element for the Midwest, and most other places, is a highway paralleling the tracks. On my

One way to check if your scene looks realistic is to place a camera on it and take a picture, as I did here.

trips through Iowa and Nebraska on the Lincoln Highway, I noticed many small, often private, grade crossings which I had good use of when I wanted to stop and watch the trains passing by. I also wanted to include one of those in my scene.

Soil and dirt

I used these homemade shakers as dirt applicators. I drilled the small holes in the lids, and the smallest applicator has smaller holes for applying very fine dirt.

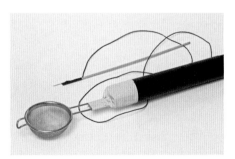

For applying static flock grass, I used this homemade grass applicator that is made from an electric flyswatter. It was a present from Kim Nipkow, a talented young modeler from Switzerland.

Dirt from my backyard, baked and sifted

Monster Modelworks Diorama Dirt

The next step is to compose the scene. With the track already in place, I placed the rest of the elements in relation to the tracks' position. First, I marked where I wanted my highway to be and then the fields. As corn seemed to be the dominate crop in Iowa and Nebraska, I decided on two cornfields and one soybean field.

An important issue is choosing scenery materials. The scenery materials are what bring a scene to life, so your choice of types and colors is essential for a good outcome. I started with the ground cover. For a basic soil, I simply used some from

Small private grade crossings are very common in rural areas, and they add to the authenticity of the scene. I made the signs and crossbucks on my computer and printed them out. The poles are stained stripwood.

my backyard that I baked in an oven for several hours to kill any living organisms hiding in it. I then sifted it so I ended up with fine-grained dirt. I wanted a lighter shade of dirt for my rural roads and discovered that Monster Modelworks offered Diorama Dirt, which had the color I was looking for.

Modeling the Midwest means using lots of grass. The days are over when you have to use colored sawdust or turf as grass. When modeling the grass-covered terrain found throughout the Midwest, and in many other places, you can either use nice-looking grass mats or the many available varieties of static flock grass. I used static flock grass for this scene. The range of brands and types you can get nowadays is almost unlimited. I didn't use just one color of grass but a mix of several shades. Even though I model summer, I actually don't use a "summer" flock grass, as I think it looks too unrealistically green.

On my research trip to Iowa and Nebraska, I also did some field studies on ballast and noticed that the color ranged from pink over uniform gray to multi-colored ballast. The multi-colored ballast seemed to be more common, so I decided that this was the type I wanted to copy for use on my mainline track. I couldn't find any commercially available scale ballast that looked like the real thing. Instead, I made my own blend from four different shades of HO scale ballast.

It's worth spending more time working with your colors, not only for ballast, but for ground cover, flock grass, and weeds. The key to having realistic-looking scenery has a lot to do with your choice of colors. Subdued colors look more realistic than very bright colors.

The finishing touch for your scenery is planting weeds, bushes, and trees. Again, your choice of colors and materials is important.

Checking the scene

A great way to check if your scene looks authentic is by taking photos of it from a low angle, as if the photo was taken by a HO scale person on your layout. I check all my scenes this way. I place a camera in various spots on the scene and take pictures.

Taken somewhere between Clarks and Silver Creek, Neb., this photo shows that mainline ballast is not always gray but instead includes many colors of rock.

I couldn't find any commercially available scale ballast that looked like the real thing, so I made my own blend from four different shades of HO scale ballast.

Mainline ballast blend

| Arizona Rock & Mineral 130-2 Northern Pacific Med Gray Granite | Arizona Rock & Mineral 138-2 CSX/Southern Pacific/ Wabash Gray | ASOA 1411 Diabasschotter | ASOA 1710 Gneisschotter |

Subterrain

Making scenery consists of various steps. Whether we are talking about desert, mountain, or Midwestern scenery, the order in which you do things is pretty much the same. Usually, the scenery construction starts right after the track has been laid, painted, and weathered.

I first apply a base for the road, which is cut from ¼" MDF board. Then I apply the subterrain. On flat land, the subterrain consists of a sheet of plywood. Even though, at first glance, the scene might look like there are no height variations, there are. I use a lightweight filler to create the sloped shoulders on the highway and smooth out any other smaller height differences. For terrain with more height variations, I use foam insulation board for the subterrain.

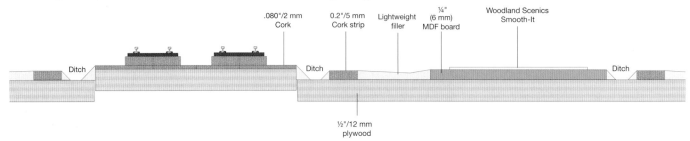

This cross section shows an area with only small height differences. I modeled these smaller height differences with lightweight filler. I add a little water to the putty until it has the consistency of whipped cream, which makes it easier to distribute evenly. I spread the putty with a piece of styrene. To prevent the putty from sticking to the styrene, I dip the styrene in water first. I glued cork strips as guides for ditches and to maintain a uniform layer of filler. You can complete this step before or after you pave the roads. It doesn't matter in which order you do these two steps.

I first applied the subroad which consists of ¼" MDF board. On the level part of the scene, I simply glued the subroad to the top of the plywood. On the other part, I attached it to risers.

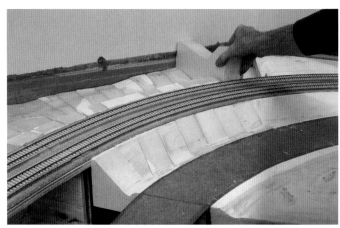

On level areas, the subterrain is just a sheet of plywood. For terrain with more height differences, I use foam insulation board. On terrain with smaller height differences, I place the sheets horizontally. On terrain with greater height differences, I cut pieces of foam sheets in shape and place them horizontally. I glued the foam with No More Nails.

Sand all the joints and cutting marks smooth with a piece of coarse sandpaper. It is a good idea to have a vacuum cleaner ready for this step.

I filled the gaps with lightweight filler, which I sanded smooth after it has dried.

After the subterrain was completed, I paved the road with a layer of Woodland Scenics Smooth-It. Details about paving roads are described on pages 64–67.

I gave the terrain a layer of earth-colored latex paint. Even though the paint will be covered with dirt and grass, it is a step you should not skip. An earth-colored base is much more forgiving than unpainted blue foam insulation and white plaster are if there are spots where the groundcover doesn't cover completely.

I also made the rural grade crossing with Smooth-It. The road has been trimmed at the grade crossing to allow space for the BLMA concrete grade crossing pieces I intended to use. It is easiest to trim the road while the plaster is still damp and softer than when it is completely dry.

After applying the earth-colored paint, I painted the road with several layers of ModelMaster Gull Gray followed by a dark wash (see page 70).

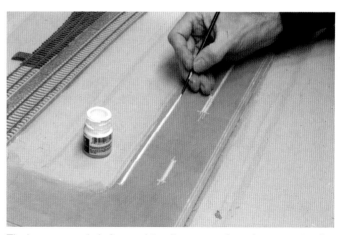

The last steps to do before applying dirt, grass, and weeds are to paint the road striping and then weather the road (see page 70).

Planting a cornfield

Most cornfields I have seen on layouts have been rather small, and I am beginning to understand why. There are several commercially produced cornstalks on the market, and some of the best looking are probably JTT's cornstalks. They come in packages of 36 single stalks, so it would take a lot of packages to cover the areas I had dedicated to cornfields. Instead, I opted for Busch cornstalks, which I think also look nice and I can obtain locally. The Busch product comes in rows of 20 stalks, which make them easier to plant than single stalks. They need some processing first, though. One package of Busch cornstalks covers a 4" × 4" square, so it still took quite a few packages, and quite a bit of money, to cover the two cornfields on this scene.

For a realistic appearance, you have to twist the leaves on each stalk in different directions. This is tedious work, and I got through it by forcing myself to process at least 10 rows every day.

To show the tassels, apply a dab of white glue to the top of the stalks and dip them in the yellow fibers included in the package.

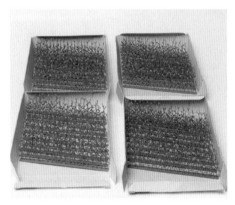

I painted the base an earth color and set them aside until I had enough plants for a field.

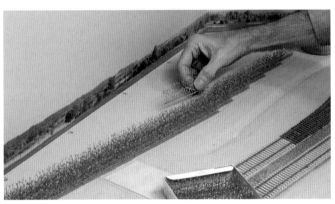

1. I attached the strips one by one to the terrain with white glue. I used white glue because if I, for some reason, wanted to remove the field, water would soften the glue, and the stalks could be reused.

2. When the planting was completed, I sprinkled fine dirt between the stalks and around the field. The dirt is from my backyard, and I baked and sifted it before using.

3. When the area had been covered with dirt, I drizzled the dirt with "wet water" (water with a little rubbing alcohol added to it). Do it carefully so you don't flush any dirt away.

4. Finally, I dripped the dirt with white glue thinned with water and left it to dry. Again, be careful not to flush the dirt away.

Applying the dirt and ballast

Even though most of the ground will be covered with grass, I still applied a layer of dirt first. I do this because no matter how thick a layer of grass fibers you apply later, it will not cover the ground completely and will leave visible spots of dirt.

Applying a base layer of ground cover consists of several steps. First, I brushed the painted surface with a thin layer of white glue thinned with water. On slopes, I use thicker glue or it will run down to the bottom of the slope before you have a chance to apply any dirt. I work on an area no bigger than 15" x 15" at one time.

1. I brushed the areas on both sides of the track with a thin layer of white glue thinned with water and then sprinkled it with dirt until everything was completely covered. I then applied a lighter shade of dirt to the dirt roads.

2. When an area has been covered with dirt, I drizzle the dirt first with wet water and then with white glue thinned with water and leave it to dry. Do it carefully so you don't flush any dirt away.

3. Apply the ballast as evenly as possible. It is easier to control if you use a spoon or a small container, such as a film canister, if anyone can remember those.

4. Use a soft, wide brush to spread out the ballast. Also wipe any ballast off the tops of the ties. To finish, I tap the top of the rails with the brush shaft to knock any remaining ballast grains off the ties.

5. To set the ballast, drizzle with wet water and then with thinned white glue (1 part glue to 2 parts water). Hold the pipette close to the ballast to keep the drops from making marks in the ballast.

6. After a few days, when everything had dried completely, I rubbed the dirt with a stiff brush to create tire marks.

Applying grass, weeds, and bushes

The choice of flock grass colors is essential for getting an authentic-looking result. Before I invested in major amounts of flock grass, I applied various brands and shades of grass fibers to a sheet of plywood coated with dirt to see how they looked under my layout's lighting. I decided on four different shades for my grass-covered terrain. Even though I model summer, I don't use "summer" grass but, instead, colors like Early Fall, Late Fall, and various beige shades. I also use different lengths: 6.5mm, 4mm, and 2mm.

I work on a small area at a time so the glue doesn't have time to dry before

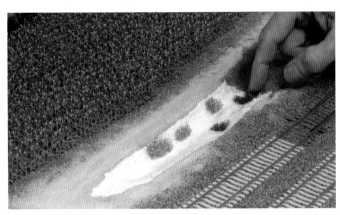

1. I brushed the area that was to receive flock grass with white glue with a little water added to it. If the glue is too thin, it will be absorbed by the dirt before you have time to apply the grass. Before I applied the grass, I planted weeds in the wet glue.

2. I applied the flock grass using a homemade grass applicator made from an electric flyswatter. I filled the sieve randomly with different shades and lengths of grass flock, stuck the counter-pole needle in the wet glue, and started shaking the applicator over the glued area.

3. I vacuumed the adjacent area clean of loose grass fibers. I placed a screen in front of the vacuum's hose, so I could save and reuse the loose fibers.

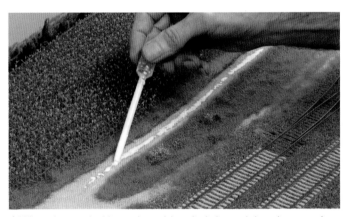

4. When the area had been cleaned, I applied glue and then the grass along the cornfield. I then vacuumed the area again and applied blobs of glue to the center of the dirt road.

5. I repeated the application of flock grass in different shades and lengths on the wet glue. I used only the shortest lengths (2–4mm) for the grass in the center of the dirt road.

6. I left the scene dry for 24 hours before vacuuming the entire area thoroughly to remove loose grass fibers.

I have covered it with weeds and grass. When applying the grass, I hold the grass applicator no higher than an inch from the ground while shaking it.

More than half of the applied grass fibers were still loose after the glue had dried, and at first, I just vacuumed them away. Later, I got the idea to place a screen in front of the vacuum cleaner's hose to collect the loose fibers and reuse them, which resulted in a drastic drop in the consumption of flock grass.

MiniNatur Grass Flock Early Fall   MiniNatur Grass Flock Late Fall   MiniNatur Grass Flock Beige   MiniNatur Grass Flock Golden Beige

Even though I model summer, I use other colors in my flock grass palette.

I use various products as weeds. From left to right are Polák Models 5979 Light Yellow Short Flowers, MiniNatur 920-21 Beech Foliage Spring, and MiniNatur 910-22 Birch Foliage Summer.

These Weed Tufts from MiniNatur are excellent for scattering around in the grass to simulate weeds. The two colors I use are 725-21 Spring and 725-22 Summer.

Small bushes and weeds were planted with a dab of white glue. The weeds I am applying are small pieces of Beech Foliage Spring from MiniNatur.

For bushes and small trees, I used Noch 23100 Nature Trees as a starting point. I believe Scenic Express makes a similar product called SuperTrees. I airbrush the bigger bushes and small trees with gray first. I dipped the top of the Nature Tree pieces in white glue thinned with water. I use ordinary white carpenter's glue thinned with water in a 1:1 ratio. I also added a little dish soap to the glue to make it flow easier around the thin branches. Finally, I sprinkled Noch 07144 Leaves Mid Green on the wet glue.

I found these flowering bushes at a train show. They are made by Polák Models.

I made these racks for holding small parts when I airbrush them, and they turned out to be very useful for holding the bushes as they dried.

Model a soybean crop

Although I model the Corn Belt, I needed another crop besides corn to add a little variety to the scenery. Soybeans are a common crop in the Corn Belt, and it turned out to be a very easy crop to model. All you need is MiniNatur grass strips, 3M Spray Mount, and some Noch Medium Green leaves.

My HO scale farmer seems to be very pleased with his new soybean field.

1. I trimmed the MiniNatur grass strips to a narrower width and then placed them on a piece of cardboard. The strips have a sticky back so they easily stick to the cardboard. I then sprayed them with 3M Display Mount.

2. I immediately sprinkled Noch leaves on the tacky glue. I let the strips dry for 24 hours before planting them on the layout. The 3M glue stays soft so the strips preserve their flexibility.

3. Using white glue, I planted the soybean rows on a piece of dirt-covered land.

This view shows the two corner sections that contain the farmland scene with corn and soybean fields.

Model realistic-looking trees

Bend and twist the Woodland Scenics plastic armature into a realistic dimensional tree shape. I also cut off the knob in the bottom of the trunk and replaced it with a piece of .028" brass wire for easier mounting on the layout.

I first painted the tree armatures light gray using an airbrush, but the paint consumption turned out to be very high, so I changed strategy and hand-painted the armatures instead. After the gray paint was dry, I gave the armatures a brown-gray wash made from Vallejo Model Air 71042 Cam Black Brown thinned with Vallejo 71161 Airbrush Thinner.

Trees have never been a big concern for me, as the locale for my previous layouts was the Mojave Desert. But now that I am modeling the Midwest, I started hunting for useful materials for making realistic-looking trees and found Noch Nature Trees. I believe Scenic Express makes a similar product called SuperTrees, I sprinkled bits of the Nature Tree product with Noch leaves and glued them to Woodland Scenics tree armatures. The result was great. The trees had just the right openness between the leaves, which gave them a very realistic look.

This is what you need to make a realistic-looking tree. Noch 23100 Nature Trees, Noch 07144 Leaves Mid Green, and Woodland Scenics TR1123 Tree Armatures. In addition, you will also need light gray paint, a brown-gray wash, white glue, and CA.

Cut the Noch Nature Trees into smaller pieces, so you have a selection of branches in various sizes and shapes. Then dip them in glue and sprinkle them with Noch leaves.

Glue the finished branches to the armature. I used a gel-type CA, and it seemed to work fine.

This scene is an example of how you can turn a practical problem into a signature scene.

Building a bridge scene

I might as well admit it right away—I like railroad bridges. There is something intriguing about watching a train cross a bridge, and I dedicated one of my layout sections to a scene containing a bridge. The bridge also serves a practical purpose. The tracks had to cross each other at some place to enter the hidden staging, and a bridge seemed like a good choice.

I wanted to incorporate water in the scene, and I visualized a scene where the lower tracks ran along a river. However, I also wanted a little forest between the high and low tracks to cover the lower tracks where they entered the hidden staging through a cutout in the backdrop. But the limited depth of the layout section didn't allow for both, so the river couldn't follow the lower tracks all the way. I had to end it halfway, so it became more like

a lake. It is one of the many compromises we model railroaders have to deal with every day, and after all, the bridge is the main object on the scene, not the river.

The railroad bridge is a Central Valley Model Works 200-foot, double-track truss bridge kit. It was not the easiest kit I have ever built. For one thing, you have to cut all the girders to correct lengths and angles. Cutting them to exact angles was a challenge—for me anyway. Central Valley Model Works offers to replace parts free of charge if you goof during assembly, which was an offer I had to take advantage of.

Two Micro Engineering deck girder bridge sections are also part of the bridge. I used bridge ties from CVMW for all the bridge sections. Besides the railroad bridge, the scene also includes a highway bridge. I chose a RIX Modern Higway Overpass kit which I built without any modifications.

Parallel with working on the subterrain, I built a Central Valley Model Works 200-foot, double-track truss bridge kit. I airbrushed the bridge with ModelMaster Burnt Sienna. There are many nooks and crannies on this structure, so it took quite a bit of paint to cover it, but CVMW cleverly made the parts of black plastic, which is a huge advantage when painting a structure like this. The walkway between the tracks are made from Plano Model Products 201 slotted .008" stainless steel sheets.

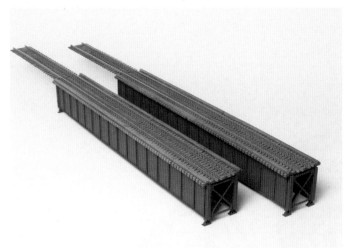

These two Micro Engineering deck girder bridge sections are also part of the bridge. I used bridge ties from CVMW for them as well. I gave the sections a coat of ModelMaster Burnt Sienna as I did on the truss bridge. I painted the ties light gray and then gave them a brown-gray wash. The rails were painted brown. Finally, I brushed the tie plates and rail with rust-colored powdered chalks.

I didn't want water clear enough that you could see the bottom of the river. I have seen a lot of green water in rivers on my trips to the Midwest so that was going to be the color of my water too. My plan was to paint the area with water green, and then apply a thin layer of resin on top of it to give it the glossy look of water.

I made the surrounding subterrain from foam insulation board. I filled all the gaps between the foam pieces with lightweight putty. Especially on the river bank where the foam insulation board joins the plywood, you have to be careful to make a 100 percent watertight seal. The area will later be filled with resin, and the resin will creep through even the slightest crack. So if you need to apply more resin to an area than you expect, it might be a good idea to take a look under the layout before you apply more.

I also applied ground cover and finished all the scenery along the riverbanks before applying the resin. I am not sure this was the smartest order to do it in, and the next time I do a scene like this, I might just apply the dirt and wait with the rest of the scenery materials until after the resin has been applied.

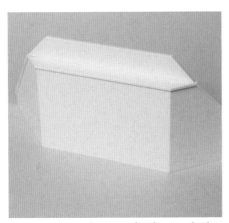

I scratchbuilt the abutments for the truss bridge and the two deck girder bridge sections from styrene.

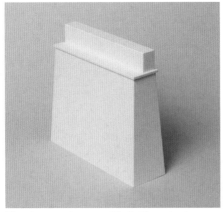

The pier was also scratchbuilt. The raised area compensates for the height difference between the truss bridge and the deck girder bridge sections.

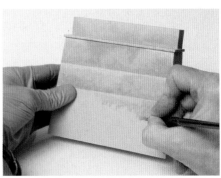

I painted the abutments and pier by first giving them a base coat of Tamiya AS-16 USAF Light Gray applied with a spray can. I then dabbed the sides and bottom randomly with two shades of gray: a light gray (ModelMaster 1732) and a darker gray mixed from 2026 Dark Drab lightened a bit with 1732 Light Gray.

This is the layout section as it looked before it was turned into a bridge scene. A sheet of plywood acts as a temporary bridge. Down in the corner, the lower track will disappear into a staging hidden behind the backdrop.

I made the subterrain from foam insulation board. I cut the pieces roughly into shape before I glued them together with No More Nails. I use various tools for cutting foam insulation board. Mostly I use a hot-wire cutter and a WS Foam Knife, but I also use an ordinary bread knife.

To be able to run trains while I was working on the section, I made as much of the terrain as I could with the temporary bridge in place.

In order to finish the subterrain, I finally had to remove the temporary bridge. I also tested to see if the Rix highway overpass included in the scene fit in the gap.

The highway bridge also needed abutments. They too were made from styrene. The white part is Evergreen .040" styrene sheet and styrene strips. The gray shelf is from a Rix highway bridge kit.

I made the highway abutment at the other end in the same way.

I attached the abutments to the layout with No More Nails. The placement of the abutments has to be very precise, so I used cardboard shims to hold each in place until the glue had dried. I made the rust streaks by brushing on powdered chalks with a damp brush.

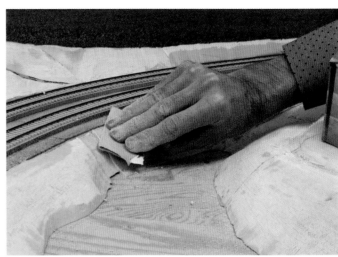

I smoothed all the joints and cutting marks with a piece of coarse sandpaper. This creates a lot of electrostatic granulate, so it is a good idea to have a vacuum cleaner ready for cleanup.

I filled the gaps between the abutment and insulation board embankment with lightweight putty.

I also filled the gap between the foam board terrain and pier, which is resting on the plywood, with lightweight putty.

I placed the bridge sections on the pier and abutments to test if it was level before I moved on to adding the scenery.

I removed the bridge sections again and applied the last few pieces on the basic terrain.

I again used lightweight putty to fill gaps between the foam insulation board sections, and was especially careful on the riverbank where the insulation board terrain joins the plywood. It needs to have a watertight seal. The area will later be filled with resin, and resin will creep through even the slightest crack.

I used a piece of medium grade sandpaper to smooth all the fillings.

The entire terrain received a base coat of earth-colored latex paint.

Before applying any ground cover I made the road, which included painting and weathering it. The methods I use for making roads are described on pages 64–71.

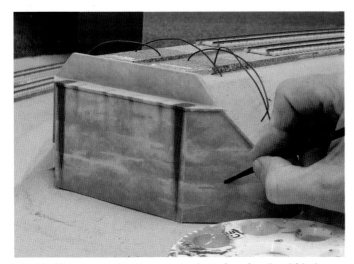

After looking at my bridge abutments and pier for a few days, I felt that the painted banding effect I had given them was too eye-catching, so I lessened it a bit.

Next, I ballasted the track. First, I sprinkled dirt on each side of the tracks. In this location, I used Diorama Dirt from Monster Modelworks. See more details about ballasting track on page 45.

I airbrushed the water area green. Relying on my memory, I mixed a green shade that looked like the water I had seen on my trip. I mixed it on the spot using Vallejo Model Air 71010 Interior Green and 71028 Sand Yellow in a ratio close to 2:1.

Applying a base layer of ground cover consists of several steps. First, I brushed a thin layer of white glue thinned with water on the painted surface. I worked on an area no bigger than 10" x 10" at a time.

Then, I sprinkled the area with dirt (baked and sifted from my backyard) until it was completely covered. I use a measuring spoon or a homemade dirt applicator made from a jar with a lid containing many small holes drilled in it. I have several of these with different sized holes in the lids, depending on how fine grained I want the dirt to be.

When the area was covered with dirt, I drizzled the dirt with wet water (water with a little rubbing alcohol added to it). Do it carefully so you don't flush any dirt away.

Then I dripped white glue thinned with water on the wet dirt. Again, be careful not to flush the dirt away.

Finally, I applied a thin top layer of dirt. I used a lighter shade of dirt for the dirt road. I then let the scene dry for a several days.

To create tire marks on the dirt road, I rubbed it with a stiff brush.

I started on the forest that covered the cutout in the backdrop where the lower tracks enter the hidden staging. Using sheets of F603 Forest Base-Late Summer from Model Scene, I first wet the back of the sheets to make them more flexible and applied them with white glue. Foam Nails from Woodland Scenics held the sheets in place until the glue had dried.

I then started applying pieces of Wild Bushes from Polák Models to the area, also attaching them with white glue. As this was my very first attempt with these scenery materials, I only worked on a small area to see how it turned out before continuing with the rest of the scene.

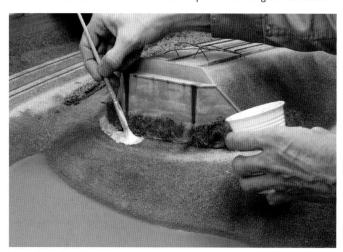

Next, I brushed the area between the dirt road and the bridge abutment with white glue thinned with a little water.

I applied flock grass using a homemade grass applicator made from an electric flyswatter. I filled the sieve randomly with different shades and lengths of grass flock, stuck the counter-pole needle in the wet glue, and started shaking the applicator over the glued area, covering it completely with grass fibers.

I repeated the procedure on the embankment, working on a small area at a time. I added less water to the glue here than I did on the embankment. If the glue is too thin, it will run down the slopes before you have time to apply the flock grass.

I filled the applicator randomly with different shades and lengths of grass flock, and started shaking the applicator over the glued area until it was completely covered with grass fibers. If you want to continue applying grass to the embankment, then vacuum the edge to remove loose grass fiber and apply glue and grass to the next section.

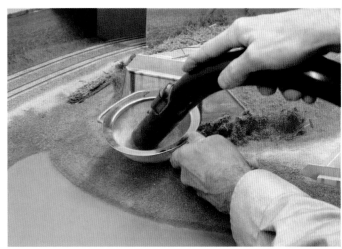

When the glue was dry, I vacuumed the area clean of loose grass fibers. I placed a screen in front of the vacuum hose to save and reuse the removed fibers.

The area between the dirt road and the riverbank was planted with Polák Wild Bushes. Each bush is attached to a rather thick mat, which I thinned with a pair of scissors. The bushes are held in place with WS foam nails while the glue is drying.

I covered the bare dirt around the wild bushes with white glue. Be aware that white glue can dissolve the glue holding the bushes, so it is a good idea not to remove the foam nails before the grass has been applied.

I then applied the grass fibers. On the area closer to the water, I used lusher and greener fibers. It can be a bit tricky to get the grass fibers under the overhang of the bushes.

After the glue had dried, I vacuumed the area to remove any loose fibers. I gently wiped the bushes with a soft brush as I held the vacuum hose close to them to get the loose fibers there.

Finally, I added larger bushes and small trees made from Bush Nature Trees. I painted them gray, dipped them in white glue thinned with water, and sprinkled them with Noch Mid Green leaves.

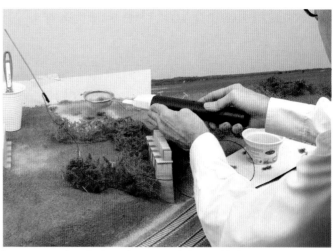

I concentrated on finishing the scenery below and behind the bridge as these areas will be difficult to access after the bridge is installed.

To be sure that the highway bridge piers were correctly positioned, I attached them to the highway bridge with rubber bands before gluing the piers to the river bottom.

After the glue dried, I removed the bridge. I then applied grass and bushes to the areas next to and below the highway bridge.

One of the piers is positioned partially on the bank. Around the posts on land, I added patches of dirt.

The larger trees in the forest behind the embankment I made as described on page 49. The smaller trees are just pieces of Noch Nature Trees with Noch leaves applied to them.

Materials used for the scenery

I used different brands of scenery materials for the scene. When you choose scenery materials, try to keep everything within the same color palette so grass, weeds, bushes, and trees blend together. This also ensures a more realistic-looking scene. I was also careful that the scenery colors matched my photographic backdrop.

The bigger trees in the scene are made from Woodland Scenics tree armatures, on which I glued pieces of Noch Nature Trees (similar to SuperTrees) that were dipped in white glue thinned with water and sprinkled with Noch leaves.

The smaller trees are just bigger pieces of Nature Trees with Noch leaves applied to them. I made these trees in two shades. Most of them I made with Mid Green leaves and a few with Dark Green leaves to break the monotony.

Polák Models Wild Bushes come in 8" x 11" (20 x 27cm) sheets. I used the colors Summer and Autumn in my scene.

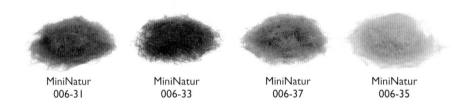

| MiniNatur 006-31 Grass Flock Spring | MiniNatur 006-33 Grass Flock Early Fall | MiniNatur 006-37 Grass Flock Beige | MiniNatur 006-35 Grass Flock Golden Beige |

These are the shades of flock grass I chose for this scene. Here, they are all 6mm, but I also used 4mm and 2mm in the same shades.

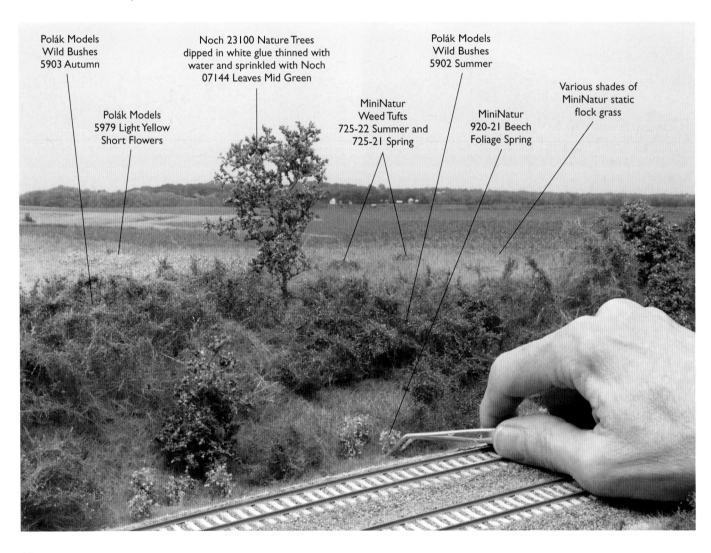

Polák Models Wild Bushes 5903 Autumn

Polák Models 5979 Light Yellow Short Flowers

Noch 23100 Nature Trees dipped in white glue thinned with water and sprinkled with Noch 07144 Leaves Mid Green

MiniNatur Weed Tufts 725-22 Summer and 725-21 Spring

Polák Models Wild Bushes 5902 Summer

MiniNatur 920-21 Beech Foliage Spring

Various shades of MiniNatur static flock grass

Working with resin

I don't have much experience in making model water. Actually, I have only tried it one time before, and then I used polyester resin, which worked fine. This time, I used an epoxy resin called Permakote, which I found in a store that sold marine supplies. Permakote is a two-part, solvent-free epoxy that hardens to a clear glass-like finish.

There are a few important procedures that you need to follow for getting good results. Pour the resin and hardener in a cup and mix it thoroughly with a stir stick.

Don't stir them but fold the resin and hardener together. Scrape the sides and bottom of the cup so all the resin is mixed with hardener. This is very important. If you have small pockets of resin that have not been mixed properly with hardener, it will leave sticky spots on the surface of your water. Work the mix for at least 3–5 minutes.

You can dye the resin with enamel paint. Apply a few drops of the color of your choice to the resin and fold it

together until the color of the mix is consistent.

Place the cup for 5 minutes on a radiator or in a jar with hot water. This makes the air bubbles in the mix rise to the surface. Then you can pour the resin. The resin should have a consistency like thick syrup, and it will take it a while to flow over the entire surface. You can help it by pushing it with the stir stick. Always wear chemical-resistant gloves when you work with resin.

I made a test batch first to see if the resin could be dyed and to see how the resin acted when I applied to an area, and I am glad I did. As you can see, the epoxy crept ¼" up the banks.

To avoid the resin from creeping up the banks, I coated them with Vallejo Matte Varnish to seal the dirt. The varnish will dry clear and be almost invisible.

I mixed the resin and hardener thoroughly. I dyed the resin by adding a few drops of Humbrol 120 and 94 to it. I poured it on the pre-painted area and distributed it with a stick. I could have applied a thicker layer, but I thought it was smarter to give it a thin layer first and see how it turned out after the resin cured. Then I could always apply another layer if necessary.

There were thousands of tiny bubbles in the resin after I poured it, but they were easy to get rid of by blowing on the surface through a straw. This makes the bubbles pop. Change straws often to avoid getting any spit in the resin. Water will haze the surface. You can also use a hair dryer to eliminate the bubbles, but only if you haven't applied grass and bushes to the banks. The hair dryer will blow any loose scenery materials in the wet resin.

I installed the railroad bridge and soldered feeder wires to the bridge tracks. Except for the two bridge shoes on the truss bridge resting on the pier, none of the sections were glued to the abutments and pier.

The walkway between the tracks is the only addition I made to the truss bridge.

Although the resin layer is only .080" (2mm) thick, it is not easy to tell how deep the water is. I applied some deadfall along the riverbank before I poured the resin.

This picture shows how nicely the various scenery materials I used in this scene complement each other.

This close-up view shows the abutment and the dirt road under the bridge.

This is an overview of the entire section. In the left corner, you can see where the lower tracks disappear into the staging.

This old highway is not in the best condition, but that wouldn't concern any railfans traveling the road. Their only worry is if there are places where they can pull over if a train comes by.

Constructing realistic streets and highways

As a railfan, I have traveled many miles on roads following trains, and since my modeling is based on what I have seen on such railfan trips, it is only natural that streets and roads have always played a big role on my layouts. Roads are wonderful scenic elements, and I use them to cut through the scenery and create viewing lines and scene dividers.

Most of us have to compress a lot of things to make them fit in the limited space we have available for our model railroad, but my roads are not one of them. I try to keep my roads and streets in a prototypically correct width. In my opinion, roads that are too narrow just don't look realistic.

Having streets and roads play such a dominate role on a layout requires that they must look realistic. I have to admit that I have not quite achieved that goal

Casting roads on a sectional layout offers some challenges you don't have on a permanent layout. At the joints between the sections, I placed a piece of waxed paper before casting the next section of the road.

grooves to the streets and sidewalks when they are made of plaster.

I use Woodland Scenics Smooth-It. This plaster is pretty easy to work with and easy to sand too. There are some rules of thumb to follow when you cast roads in plaster. The thinner you make the mix, the greater the risk for having air bubbles in it. And a thicker mix is more difficult to spread evenly because the plaster has a tendency to stick to the spreader. To compensate for these undesirable side effects, I usually first apply a thick mix to an area, and when the plaster has set but not dried, I apply a thin top layer of thin plaster to smoothen out the worst irregularities.

Asphalt can be many colors—from almost black to brown and shades of tan and gray, so you need to study the roads' colors in the location you are modeling. I paint the plaster roads with enamel paint. I thin the paint so it ends up almost like a wash and apply it in 4–5 layers. I let each layer dry completely before applying the next layer. The first layer will be absorbed by the plaster and act like a primer and seal the surface. You can add road markings and striping with decals, but I prefer to paint them. Painted stripes have a less clean and more realistic look.

Streets and roads are never clean, so you need to weather them to make them completely realistic. I use a combination of stains and powdered chalks to weather the road surface.

on my previous layouts, so building on experiences from my previous layouts, I decided to make an extra effort to make my streets and roads look realistic this time.

I prefer making my streets and highways from plaster. I have tried using styrene

sheets for streets, but it just doesn't work for me. Even after the styrene has been painted and weathered, the surface still doesn't have a realistic concrete or asphalt feel to it. Plaster roads have a slightly non-uniform surface which, to me, looks very realistic. It is also easy to apply cracks and

Casting plaster highways, streets, and sidewalks

1. To create an even surface for the plaster pavement, I first made subroads from ¼" MDF board. On flat areas, I simply screwed the MDF sheets directly to the plywood surface. On more uneven terrain, I attached the subroad to risers.

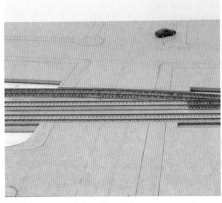

2. Using a pencil, I outlined the streets and sidewalks for the town scene. I used a model vehicle as a reference to get the proportions right.

3. I elevated the areas for buildings slightly by gluing pieces of .080" cork to the base. In areas where there are no buildings, I applied WS Paving Tape (a foam tape approximately .060" thick) along the outside edges of the streets.

4. I started by paving the main street. I mixed a small portion of Smooth-It with water and poured it along the track at the grade crossing.

5. I spread the plaster with a piece of styrene, using the top of the rail as a guide. Avoid getting plaster too close to the rail.

6. I then mixed a bigger batch of plaster and poured it on the rest of the street. The two pieces of cork across the side streets are just temporary. They are needed so the plaster will maintain the same thickness all over when it is spread.

7. I spread the plaster with a wide piece of styrene. The plaster on the styrene spreader tends to build up and stick to it, which can make it difficult to spread it evenly. This problem can be alleviated by dipping the styrene spreader in water first.

8. After the main street had been covered with plaster, I applied some to the areas between the tracks at the grade crossing.

9. Spread it carefully and make sure the plaster doesn't cover too much of the ties or, even worse, the rail.

10. I continued spreading the plaster until I reached the other side of the tracks.

11. In the meantime, the plaster on the main street had set but was still damp, and this is the perfect time for adding a top layer to smoothen out any dips in the surface. For the top layer, I use a thinner mix of plaster than the one I used for the base layer.

12. The thin plaster mix spreads evenly with the styrene spreader. Don't add any pressure to the spreader, just let it ride on top of the wet plaster.

13. When the plaster had set but not dried, I removed the temporary cork pieces across the side streets.

14. The side streets are made the exact same way as the main street, so I repeated this procedure.

15. I spread the plaster, moving from the edge of the layout section towards the main street.

16. Where the side street connects to the main street, I used a smaller spreader to smoothen the joint between the two streets. I made the side street while the plaster on the main street was still damp. If you don't cast both streets consecutively so the plaster has had time to dry, then you need to wet it at the joint or the dry plaster will absorb the moisture from the wet plaster, which will make it difficult to create a smooth joint.

17. The road had to be trimmed at the grade crossing. I cut along a homemade styrene template and removed the excess plaster. The template is slightly wider than the BLMA concrete grade crossing pieces I intended to use for this grade crossing. It is easiest to trim the road while the plaster is still damp and softer than when it is completely dry.

18. After a couple of days, when the plaster had dried completely, I removed the foam tape and sanded the surface. If the surface is very irregular, you can use a power sander but be careful if you do. A power sander is very effective and you can easily sand off too much of the plaster before you know it. The sanding often reveals small holes created by air bubbles in the surface. To repair them, I wet the area and filled them with a little plaster.

19. The next step is casting sidewalks. I applied WS Paving Tape, a foam tape approximately .060" thick, along the outside edge of the sidewalks, but first I wiped the areas along the sidewalks completely free of plaster dust from the sanding. The easiest was is to wipe it away with a damp cloth. Even the slightest bit of dust will prevent the tape from adhering to the surface.

20. Before I applied the plaster, I brushed the dry plaster surface with water. If you don't wet the dry plaster first, it will instantly absorb the moisture from the wet plaster and leave you without any time to smooth it out.

21. I filled the area between the tape strips with plaster. When pouring the plaster, try to get as close as possible to the exact amount needed to fill an area. Applying too much plaster makes it difficult to spread without pushing some over the edge of the foam tape.

22. Spread the plaster evenly with a piece of styrene. Avoid getting any on the street. If any gets on the dry plaster, remove it instantly. As on the streets, I added a second layer of plaster to the walkways right after the first layer had set.

23. All the sidewalks are cast and left to dry. I don't remove the foam tape before the plaster is completely dry, which takes 24 hours and sometimes longer, depending on the humidity in the room.

24. I sanded the sidewalks smooth. The edge of the curb was sanded round. At the downtown crossroads, I sanded the sidewalk level with the street.

25. I outlined the driveways with paving tape and filled them with Smooth-It. I wet the dry plaster where the driveway joins the sidewalk to prevent the dry plaster from sucking all the moisture out of the wet plaster when it is applied.

26. I made styrene foundations for the town buildings and filled the areas between them with plaster to create a back alley.

27. With a pencil, I outlined the slabs on the streets and sidewalks. I scratched the grooves with a pointed tool using a ruler as guide. I also made a few cracks in the street using the same tool.

Painting concrete streets

1. I gave the concrete sidewalks and streets a coat of a extra-light concrete color mixed from Humbrol 147 Light Gray, 34 White, and 121 Pale Stone in a 2:2:1 ratio. I used a light color because the streets will receive a dark wash later that will darken the surface. I made the paint pretty thin, almost like a wash. Because the paint is so thin, the plaster will absorb the first layer which will act like a primer and seal the plaster surface.

2. After the first layer had dried, I sanded the surface lightly with very fine sandpaper. I then gave streets and sidewalks a second layer of the thin concrete color. I applied four layers to the streets before I was pleased with the look. I sanded between each layer. You get a more realistic-looking surface by giving plaster streets several layers of thin paint instead of one or two layers of a thicker and more opaque paint.

3. I sanded the painted streets and sidewalks and cleaned the surface of dust. I then gave the surface a dark wash (a few drops of Vallejo Air 71052 German Gray mixed with water and a little rubbing alcohol). This will bring out the grooves and cracks in the surface but will also leave the gray color less uniform.

4. I masked the outside edge of the road markings and painted them by hand. Always rub the edges of the masking tape to prevent paint from creeping under it. I wanted the road markings to look old and faded, so I only gave them a single layer of paint. Newer striping gets two layers of paint.

5. I sealed the road surface with a coat of Vallejo Matte Varnish. I covered the backdrop with a piece a cardboard to protect it from spray.

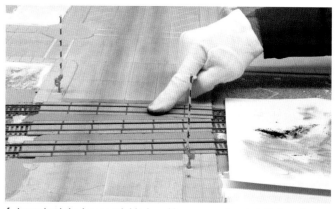

6. I smudged the lanes with black and brown powdered chalk. I used a "weathering glove," a white butler's glove. I dipped my forefinger in powder and wiped it partially clean on a sheet of paper before rubbing it on the street. I then used the clean fingers to smooth out the powder.

Finishing paved highways

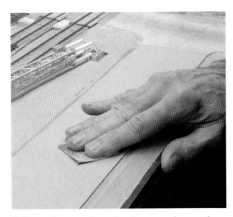

1. I gave the paved roads a light gray base color (ModelMaster Gull Gray). As on the concrete roads, I applied the color in several thin layers. When the paint was dry, I sanded the surface with fine sandpaper.

2. I lightened the edges of the road by airbrushing them with ModelMaster Sand (⅔) and white (⅓).

3. I then brushed the surface with the same dark wash I used for the concrete roads (a few drops Vallejo Air 71052 German Gray mixed with water and a little rubbing alcohol).

4. Before masking the areas for road striping, I sealed the road surface with Vallejo Matte Varnish. I don't know if this step was necessary, but I was afraid that the masking tape would pull off the dark stain when it was removed.

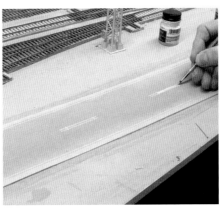

5. I masked the outside edge of the road markings. I painted the center lines yellow and the line along the edge of the road white. I applied the lines in two light coats. The center lines are 10 scale feet long and the space between them is 30 scale feet.

6. I smudged the lanes with black and brown powdered chalk. As I did on the concrete streets, I used my "weathering glove."

7. To make the dark areas more irregular, I worked on them with a damp cloth.

8. Finally, I painted on cracks using a dark gray color and a fine brush.

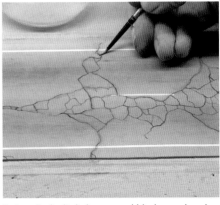

9. I applied a little brown and black powdered chalk along the largest crack and smudged it with a fine brush dipped in water.

This top view of the concrete city streets shows how modeling them in a proper width provides a more authentic look.

The final touch in finishing the roads is adding highway signs. I created them on my computer and printed them out on a label sheet. I applied the peel-and-stick signs to a sheet of .010" styrene, cut them out, and glued them to poles.

The highway parallels the track on most of the layout.

A look down the main street of Daneburg shows how a backdrop extends a scene far beyond the layout's actual physical space. Only seven of the buildings in the picture are models.

Modeling a Midwestern town

A small town, not to mention a city, takes up a lot of layout space, even if you only model part of one. On larger layouts, where you are not as restricted with space, it is easier to model an authentic-looking town than on a small layout like mine, but there are ways to limit the amount of structures used and still maintain an illusion of a town. My town only consists of a few stores and a small residential area with three homes.

Every town has a main street, and mine does too. Instead of having it run parallel with the tracks, I turned my main street 90 degrees and let it cross the track. That way, I only had to place a few buildings

on each side of the street. The backdrop would compensate for the rest.

For the scene, I simply took a photo of a typical small-town main street, had it printed out, and applied it to the backdrop. On a photo, the illusion is perfect, but when you stand looking at the enlarged scene on the backdrop, you have to view it from the right angle for it to work best.

Even though Cornerstone, DPM, and other manufacturers offer a large selection of typical Midwestern small-town buildings to choose from, only a few of the structures in my town are commercial kits. The rest are scratchbuilt buildings based on prototypes I photographed on a

research trip to Iowa and Nebraska. They are not all from the same town though. I stopped in many small towns and took pictures of buildings I thought would make a nice model. As I did, I also looked for main streets that I could photograph and use as a backdrop.

The high percentage of scratchbuilt buildings gives the town an authentic look. Had I only used commercial kits, the risk is that the viewers would recognize them and see Cornerstone and DPM buildings rather than the small Midwestern town of Daneburg.

I scratchbuilt my buildings from a variety of materials. Most of them are

The scratchbuilt structures in my layout's town are all based on actual buildings that I found on my research trip to Iowa and Nebraska. For example, the Daneburg Quick Stop is based on a grocery store in Blairstown, Iowa. To make it fit a vacant lot in my town, I modified my version by making it a little wider than the prototype.

I made this concrete block garage from basswood. Wood would normally not be my first choice for a concrete block building, but I wanted to try the laser-engraved concrete block basswood sheets from Monster Modelworks. I was a bit sceptical that it would be possible to make wood look like concrete blocks, but the final result turned out quite well.

Many of us have boxes full of leftovers from kits and scratchbuilding projects, in which you can find useful parts like doors, windows, vents, etc., for projects, but your scrap box may also contain enough parts to build an entire structure. I designed Seline's Hair Parlor around parts I had in my scrap box, and in doing so, built a no-cost structure.

made from styrene, but you will also find buildings made from basswood, laser-cut wood, or a combination of materials. Smaller scratchbuilding projects like my small town's houses give you an excellent opportunity to try out different types of materials and compare the results.

I didn't glue the buildings to their foundations because I wanted them to be easy to remove in case I later want to apply interior details to them or replace some of them with new buildings.

This photo of the main street of a typical Midwestern small town is attached to the backdrop and reminds me of a setting in a Hollywood studio.

In this view east on Railroad Street, the Daneburg Quick Stop is on the left and behind it is the Railroad Cafe, which is built from one of the few kits I used for constructing my town.

For a typical, small-town residential area, you need typical small-town homes, and fortunately, Laser-Art structures offer a nice selection of wood kits for such homes. They are easy to build, and you can build them as instructed or modify them to suit your needs.

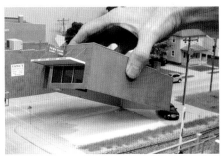

None of the buildings are attached to their styrene foundations with glue, so they can be removed easily if needed.

The pawn shop is another example of a building based on a prototype and scratchbuilt from styrene.

Alleys and the rear of buildings are just as important to model as the front sides.

As you can see in this birds-eye view of my town, it consists of only eight buildings and three homes. It's probably a little bit short of what is needed to model a town, but that was what I had room for.

Building a small-town building from styrene

Building a structure from scratch has the advantage that you can design it to fit any available space on your layout. In addition, you also get an unique structure. I built this former store, which now houses an insurance agency, entirely from styrene. In many ways, styrene is an easy material to work with. It is easy to cut and glue. It also comes in sheets having many different patterns to choose from. I used a Walthers Cornerstone styrene sheet with a brick pattern for this structure. I found that these styrene walls were tougher to cut. Unlike the white Evergreen styrene, you can't just make a few cuts and then break

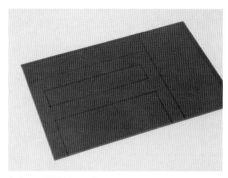

1. I used Walthers Cornerstone styrene brick sheets (933-3522) for the walls. I started by outlining the various wall sections with a pen. Be aware that the brick pattern must match where the sections join. The outlined section here is the front wall.

2. I cut out the sections with a scalpel. The styrene is tough to cut so you have to make many strokes to cut all the way through the material. I made the first cuts along a steel ruler and then deepened them freehand. I sanded all the edges smooth using fine sandpaper.

3. The finished front wall section consists of several pieces glued together with styrene cement. There is trim at the top, a recessed area on the wall, and openings for the store windows and door.

4. In this close-up of the front wall details, you can see the top trim and recessed area.

5. I beveled the corner edges on all wall sections at a 45-degree angle. I first roughly trimmed them with a scalpel and then sanded them smooth.

6. When I cut out the openings for the doors and windows, I drilled a series of holes inside the openings first and then removed the material. This makes it easier to cut the opening as the styrene will be flexible and not bind against the blade when you cut.

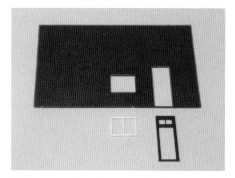

7. The rear wall section is ready with openings for the window and door frames. The door frame is from Grandt Line, and the window frame is from Rix Products.

8. i prepared the side wall sections. The narrow pieces are for the inside walls above the roof.

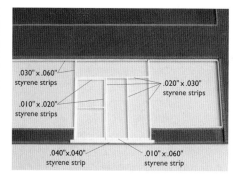

9. I made the front window and door frames from various styrene strips. I first glued the four long vertical strips in place and then the horizontal strips. After that, I attached the two vertical strips next to the door.

the sheet. If you try that method with the Walthers brick styrene sheets, you will not get a clean break but a very rough and uneven edge. You have to cut all the way through with a sharp knife, which takes many cuts.

My building is not an exact replica of a specific prototype, but it is based on several common buildings found in small towns throughout the Midwest. The structure's dimensions are $4^{1}/_{3}$" (110mm) wide, 6" (152mm) deep, and $3^{15}/_{64}$" (82mm) high.

As with most other models, a high-quality paint job can elevate the appearance of the structure. I used a combination of airbrushing and drybrushing to transform this relatively uninteresting building into one of the more eye-catching structures on my layout.

10. I reinforced the corners with square styrene strips. I also inserted styrene triangles to keep the corners at an exact 90-degree angle.

11. I cut trim from .010" styrene and glued it to the top edge of the walls. I used a .020" styrene sheet to make the roof. To simulate tar paper, I applied self-adhesive paper cut in 4-scale-foot-wide strips to the roof.

12. I painted everything light gray and then drybrushed the bricks a brick color (Humbrol 70 mixed with 237). I left the trim and window frames light gray. (Drybrushing is a technique in which you wipe most of the paint off the brush on a piece of paper before it touches the model. That way, only the bricks get paint and the mortar stays gray. Use a flat brush.)

13. This close-up of the brick wall shows the really nice brick effect you get from drybrushing, and the best thing is, is that the technique is surprisingly easy to do. After the bricks were painted, I gave the walls a coat of flat varnish applied with an airbrush.

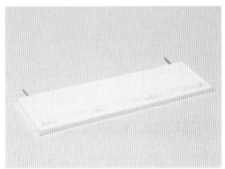

14. The awning consists of a .040" styrene sheet with .010" x .100" styrene strips attached to the edge. The two brass pins are mounting pins that fit into corresponding holes in the store's front. I painted it the same light gray I used for the rest of the building.

15. I airbrushed the roof with ModelMaster Gunship Gray mixed with Skin Tone Dark Tint (3:1). The air conditioner is from a Walthers roof detail kit (933-3733). The silver stack I made from pieces of styrene rod and tube. I applied tinted film to the glazing before attaching the glazing to the model with MicroScale Kristal Kleer. The support for the awning is .019" brass wire. I made the signs on my computer and printed them out with my printer.

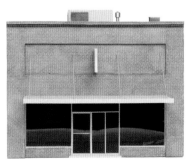

Although my grain elevator facility is heavily compressed, it still looks impressive as it dwarfs the hoppers.

Building a signature structure

A grain elevator of some kind is a must when you model the Heartland, and my plan was to have the grain elevator be the signature structure on my layout. I dedicated almost an entire layout section to the grain elevator scene.

You can purchase many nice grain elevator and silo kits, but I wanted my grain facility to be a little out of the ordinary, so I went on a research trip through Iowa and Nebraska following U.S. 30 in hopes of finding a prototype that I could base my model on.

Every town I went through had a grain elevator, and they were all so big that any I modeled would have to be compressed quite a bit to fit on my layout. Especially when you model tall structures such as grain elevators, you can get away with

selective compression without it being too obvious. That's because your eye is pretty good at seeing horizontal spaces but not very good at judging vertical spaces, so when you looking at an actual grain elevator, it seems smaller than it really is.

I ended up choosing the grain facility in Lexington, Neb., as an inspiration for my model. What made that facility more interesting than others was that you could tell it had grown over the years. A cluster of concrete silos represented the original grain elevator. Then at some point, a couple of corrugated steel storage bins had been added to the facility. A third addition featured two fairly new, modern concrete storage silos. I thought that a grain elevator like that, which had been expanded over the years, would be an

interesting model for my modern era layout.

When I built a cement plant for my previous layout, I learned how time consuming it can be to build large structures from scratch, so this time, my thought was to do as much as I could using commercial kits, either by using them as they were or by kitbashing.

This meant that my grain facility would not be an exact copy of the one in Lexington—a compromise I was willing to accept. After all, I was modeling a fictitious place and not Lexington It was not possible to build an authentic-looking grain facility from kits alone. Some of the structure sections, or parts of them, had to be scratchbuilt. But using the commercial parts, as well as parts from my scrap box (a box containing leftovers from plastic kits I have built during my 20 years in the hobby) came in handy.

I am not able to provide every exact detail in the building process, but I can give you a description with enough details that hopefully will make it possible for you to build something similar.

I basically built the structure in chronological order, starting with the concrete silos in the middle, then the steel storage bins, and ending with the two modern concrete silos. I used Walthers kits as base for both types of concrete silos and the steel storage bins.

The steel storage bins were pretty easy to make, as the Walthers kit matched the bins on the prototype. They did need a few modifications though. The reinforcement system and platforms on the bins were made of strip styrene. I used one-and-a-half kits per bin to give them a more accurate height. The biggest problem with using commercial kits for a grain facility is that the bins and silos are much too small, but making them just a half section taller made a huge difference in their appearance. I built the silo section from Walthers kits, and also adjusted their height by extending them by half a section.

One thing that will ruin the look of a structure is having ladders and handrails that are too heavy, so I used etched brass caged ladders for the entire facility, and made most handrails from scratch using .020" x .020" styrene strips.

Styrene is my favorite material for scratchbuilding, and I used it for finishing most of the structure. It is easy to cut and glue. You can find strips in almost any dimension and shape, and a variety of sheets are available that will suit most needs.

You only need a few tools for working with styrene: a sharp hobby knife or a scalpel, a razor saw, and fine sandpaper. I primarily use a scalpel for cutting styrene. When you divide a styrene sheet into smaller pieces, you don't need to cut all the way through, but can break the styrene after a few cuts. Styrene sheets from Evergreen especially have a very clean and straight edge when it breaks. Cutting out window and other openings gets a little more complicated. I start by making multiple cuts, using a steel ruler

This grain elevator in Lexington, Neb., was the inspiration for my grain facility.

as a guide, at all four sides until the knife has gone all the way through. For making very small openings, it is easiest to remove most of the material in the opening first by drilling holes in it and then trimming the opening's edge with a knife. For cutting parts from thicker styrene, I use a razor saw.

For gluing styrene, I use Tamiya Extra Thin Cement. You simply hold the parts together and apply the cement along the joint with a brush. The cement will flow in the joint by itself, leaving hardly any visible trace of glue. For gluing metal to styrene, I use a gel type cyanoacrylate adhesive (CA).

I didn't go crazy with the detailing of the structure. I wanted to capture the overall look and feeling of a big grain elevator, so I applied only the details necessary to accomplish that. Then, one day when my layout is completely finished, I can always add more details if I feel like it. If you want to model every detail seen on the prototype of a big complex structure like this, it may take more time to finish than you have available for the hobby.

What really makes a structure like this come to life and appear authentic is the painting and weathering. I custom-mixed almost all the shades used to paint the

various parts of the structure. Be aware that a color looks darker on a bigger surface, so you almost always need to mix a lighter shade than you think. Colors also look very different under a layout's artificial light than they do under bright sunlight, so you have to adjust for that as well. The colors even looked slightly different under my workbench light compared to how they looked under the layout's fluorescent lamps. Test your colors on a sheet of styrene before you paint the structure.

I learned an important lesson from building the cement plant for my previous layout: make each section in subassemblies that can be painted separately. I didn't do that on the cement plant and that made the masking and painting extremely complicated and time consuming. This time, each section had several subassemblies, so painting them in different colors required a minimum of masking.

Silo section

I made the silo section from three Walthers grain silo kits (933-2942). The prototype silos consist of a cluster of 3 rows of 4 silos, 12 silos in total. I wanted a slimmer structure, and my version consists of two rows of six silos instead.

The silos in the Walthers kit are not very tall, so I extended the silo sections with a half section. The biggest challenge was to make a totally straight cut where I cut the sections I needed for the extension in halves.

I needed half silo sections for the extension. First, I marked a cutting line. Place the silo section up against something stable. In this case, I used a sanding stone. I had made a ruler the exact half-length of a section. I placed the ruler up against the sanding stone and drew a line across the silo section.

After the glue on the extended sections had dried completely, I sanded them smooth. Here, you can see an untreated section next to a sanded section. The joint becomes almost invisible after sanding.

At the corners, there is a visible seam where the end sections join the other sections. To get rid of the seam, I glued a thin strip of styrene to the seam. Then I applied plenty of thin cement—so much that it started dissolving the styrene strip. I pressed the softened styrene strip into the seam and let it dry.

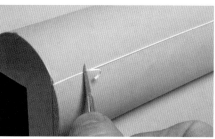

I trimmed the styrene strip flush with the silo and sanded it smooth.

I cut the sections in half with a razor saw.

I cut two silo top sections to size and glued them together before attaching the top to the silos. The top edge had an uneven overhang, which I trimmed flush with the silos.

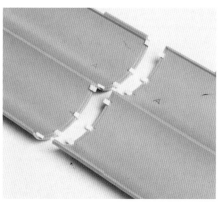

I glued small styrene tabs to the ends of the silo sections where they join. The tabs will interlock and create a exact join of the two sections. I pushed the sections together, and sealed the joint with thin plastic cement.

I glued the silo sections together and then to the base, which I made from two bases to fit the row of six silos.

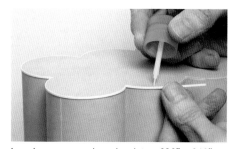

I made a new overhang by gluing .020" x .060" styrene strips to the edge.

Fall protection rack

To meet OSHA (Occupational Safety and Health Administration) requirements for keeping workers from falling off the top of the cars, I made this fall protection rack for the HO scale workers to hook their harnesses to.

The fall protection rack had to be built from scratch, which wasn't a problem as it can be built from Evergreen styrene strips. The rack was going to be a different color than the silos, so I didn't glue it to the silos yet.

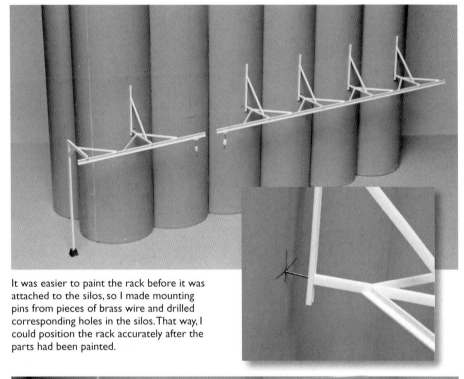

It was easier to paint the rack before it was attached to the silos, so I made mounting pins from pieces of brass wire and drilled corresponding holes in the silos. That way, I could position the rack accurately after the parts had been painted.

Fall protection systems are seen on most grain elevators nowadays.

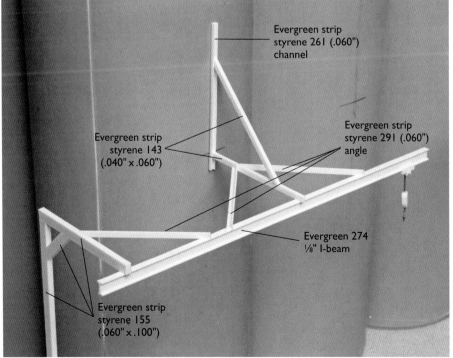

Evergreen strip styrene 261 (.060") channel

Evergreen strip styrene 143 (.040" x .060")

Evergreen strip styrene 291 (.060") angle

Evergreen 274 ⅛" I-beam

Evergreen strip styrene 155 (.060" x .100")

I made the two self-retracting lifeline systems from pieces of .060" x .100" styrene cut and sanded into shape. The attachments to the beam were each made from three pieces of 261 (.060") channel. The hook and wire were shaped from pieces of brass wire.

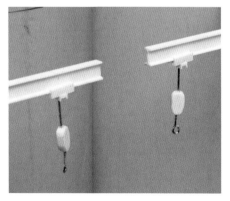

Hopper loading station

Some structures had to be built from scratch, and the hopper loading station was one of them.

On a sheet of thick paper, I drew the outlines of the structure seen from the front and also from the side, so I could figure out what the exact size of the parts would be. I also marked where the track center was and outlined the cross section of a grain hopper, so I could place the hopper filling tube exactly above the hopper's hatches.

I glued the I-beam frame sections together on top of my drawing, which also served as a template. I placed a steel ruler on the template as a straight edge to ensure the parts were properly lined up.

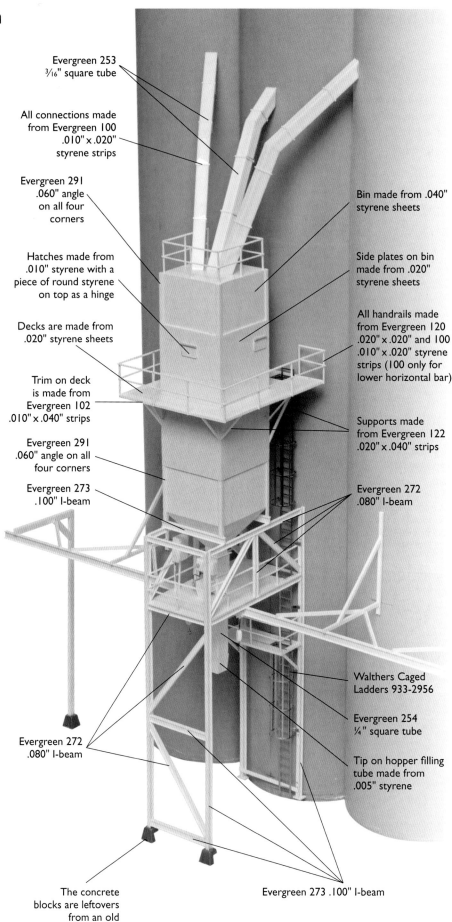

Evergreen 253
³⁄₁₆" square tube

All connections made from Evergreen 100 .010" x .020" styrene strips

Evergreen 291 .060" angle on all four corners

Hatches made from .010" styrene with a piece of round styrene on top as a hinge

Decks are made from .020" styrene sheets

Trim on deck is made from Evergreen 102 .010" x .040" strips

Evergreen 291 .060" angle on all four corners

Evergreen 273 .100" I-beam

Evergreen 272 .080" I-beam

Bin made from .040" styrene sheets

Side plates on bin made from .020" styrene sheets

All handrails made from Evergreen 120 .020" x .020" and 100 .010" x .020" styrene strips (100 only for lower horizontal bar)

Supports made from Evergreen 122 .020" x .040" strips

Evergreen 272 .080" I-beam

Walthers Caged Ladders 933-2956

Evergreen 254 ¼" square tube

Tip on hopper filling tube made from .005" styrene

The concrete blocks are leftovers from an old Walthers pipe kit

Evergreen 273 .100" I-beam

Like the other parts of the grain facility, I didn't model an exact copy of the hopper loading station but compressed and simplified it quite a bit.

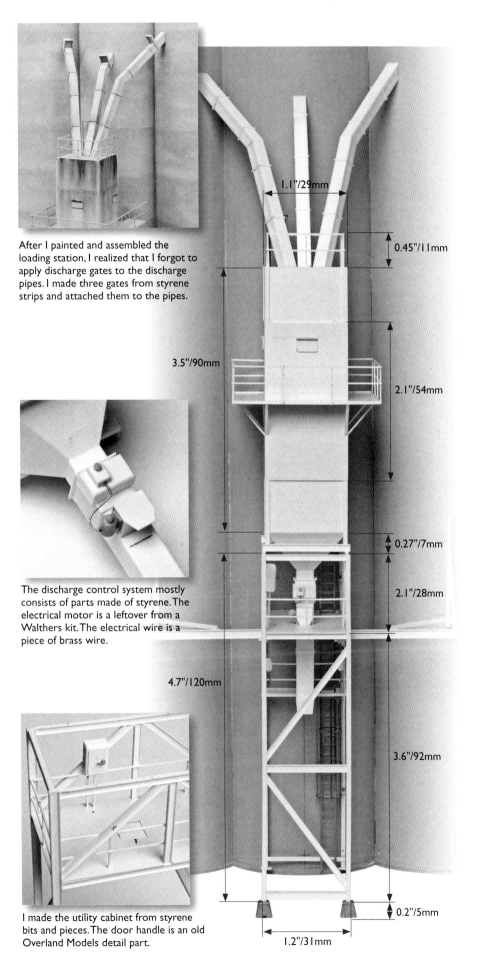

After I painted and assembled the loading station, I realized that I forgot to apply discharge gates to the discharge pipes. I made three gates from styrene strips and attached them to the pipes.

The discharge control system mostly consists of parts made of styrene. The electrical motor is a leftover from a Walthers kit. The electrical wire is a piece of brass wire.

I made the utility cabinet from styrene bits and pieces. The door handle is an old Overland Models detail part.

1.1"/29mm

0.45"/11mm

3.5"/90mm

2.1"/54mm

0.27"/7mm

2.1"/28mm

4.7"/120mm

3.6"/92mm

0.2"/5mm

1.2"/31mm

I made the hopper loading station as two separate sections so it was easier to paint.

I airbrushed the loading station with the color I mixed for the bins (ModelMaster 1732 Light Gray and 2105 French Dark Blue in a 2:1 ratio) but added about 50 percent MM 1733 Camouflage Gray to lighten it. The rust spots are dry powdered chalk (Dark Rust and Black) mixed with flat varnish and brush-painted on. The streaks are powdered chalks (Light Rust, Medium Rust, and Dark Rust) applied with a soft brush.

Conveyor legs and distributing pipes

Modeling conveyor legs is fortunately easy, as Walthers offers kits for two different versions. I had to use multiple kits for each leg because mine had to be taller than the conveyor leg the kit built.

I improved the looks of the conveyor leg by adding brass ladders, scratchbuilding platforms and handrails, and using brass micro mesh for all walkways.

The distributing bin and distributing pipe system had to be built from scratch as, to my knowledge, they are not available in kits.

I also scratchbuilt the horizontal conveyor system on top of the silos.

The tops of the prototype silos look very busy, and I was not able to tell from my prototype photos how everything was constructed and connected, so I had to both simplify and improvise. Even though I simplified my silos a lot on top, they still looked pretty busy.

To make painting the structure easier, I didn't permanently attach the elevators, conveyor, distributing bin with distributing pipes, and walkways to the silo. I created a system with mounting pins and corresponding holes, so everything could easily be taken apart and assembled again.

The authentic appearance of the silo section has a lot to do with the painting and weathering. The biggest challenge was to re-create the look of old concrete. I used a dabbing technique I developed back when I painted game figures with my son, and it worked just as well for silos as it did for dragons.

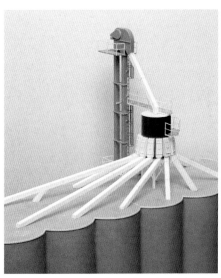

The distributing piping from the selector head leads to the silos. I made them from Evergreen 253 ³⁄₁₆" square tube. The pipes must run at a constant slope to make the grain flow.

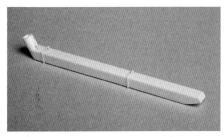

Each discharge pipe is made from ³⁄₁₆" square tube with a piece of round ³⁄₁₆" tube glued to the end that connects to the selector head. The connections between the pipe sections are made from Evergreen 100 .010" x .020" styrene strips.

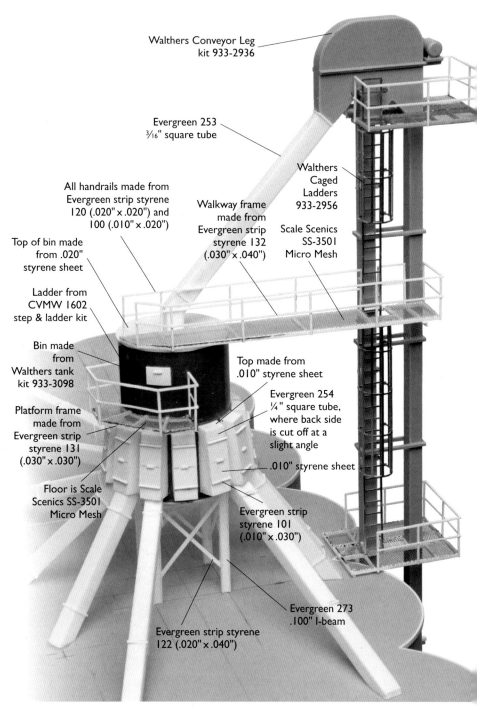

Walthers Conveyor Leg kit 933-2936

Evergreen 253 ³⁄₁₆" square tube

Walthers Caged Ladders 933-2956

All handrails made from Evergreen strip styrene 120 (.020" x .020") and 100 (.010" x .020")

Walkway frame made from Evergreen strip styrene 132 (.030" x .040")

Scale Scenics SS-3501 Micro Mesh

Top of bin made from .020" styrene sheet

Ladder from CVMW 1602 step & ladder kit

Top made from .010" styrene sheet

Evergreen 254 ¼" square tube, where back side is cut off at a slight angle

Bin made from Walthers tank kit 933-3098

.010" styrene sheet

Platform frame made from Evergreen strip styrene 131 (.030" x .030")

Evergreen strip styrene 101 (.010" x .030")

Floor is Scale Scenics SS-3501 Micro Mesh

Evergreen 273 .100" I-beam

Evergreen strip styrene 122 (.020" x .040")

I used the top platform from the Walthers conveyor leg kit, but I removed most of the ribs from the top platform and applied Scale Scenics SS-3501 Micro Mesh instead. I didn't use the handrails that came with the kit because they looked a tad too heavy. Instead, I made new ones from Evergreen .020" x .020" and .010" x .020" strip styrene.

The tall elevator to the left was made the same way as the other by using a Walthers Conveyor Leg kit 933-2936 beefed up with brass caged ladders and micro mesh walkways. For the center elevator, I used the top from an elevator included in Walthers Corn Storage Silo and Elevator kit 933-2975. The legs were made from Evergreen 187 .125" x .156" strips sandwiched between .156" wide strips cut from a .010" styrene sheet.

A top view of the completed elevator shows the walkways and distributing pipe arrangement.

I made everything as separate sections that can be taken apart, so painting would be easier—a lesson I learned when I built a cement plant for my previous layout. I applied guiding pins made of brass wire to each section and drilled corresponding holes in the silos.

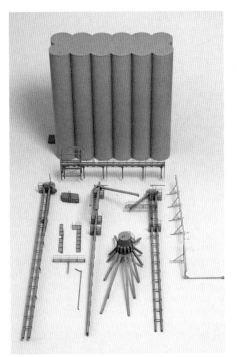

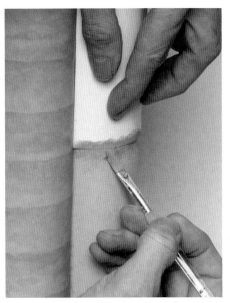

I gave the silos several coats with a Tamiya spray can (AS-16 USAF Light Gray). Then I airbrushed the conveyor legs, selector head, and other parts gray (ModelMaster 1732 Light Gray and 2105 French Dark Blue in a 2:1 ratio). The fall protection rack was airbrushed with Model Master 1569 Flat Yellow toned down with white and a little light gray.

Of course, painting the silos involved more than just spraying on the light gray Tamiya paint. Old concrete silos are anything but uniform gray, and I tried to reproduce that look by dabbing the surface with a dark warm gray (ModelMaster 1730 Flat Gull Gray with some 2125 Russian Earth added to it) and a light gray (ModelMaster 1733 Camouflage Gray and 1768 White at a 1:1 ratio). The effect is surprisingly lifelike.

To produce the horizontal banding effect, I held a piece of paper against the silo before painting each section. The horizontal banding is caused from the way the silo is built. The forms are filled with concrete, the concrete sets, and then the form is moved up to begin the process again. Each batch of concrete displays a slightly different color to give the banded effect.

I weathered the conveyor legs, other top details, and the fall protection rack by dusting them with a light gray wash applied with an airbrush. The rack also received some rust-colored powdered chalk. After I completed the painting and weathering, I assembled everything and secured it with CA.

I also modeled, painted, and weathered the back side of the silos even though none of it will be visible, but you never know if one day you will use the grain elevator in a different context where the back side will be visible.

Storage bins

The two corrugated steel grain storage bins for my grain facility are basically Walthers Grain Bin kits 933-3123. It doesn't take much to modify these bins to make a more unique structure. First you need to make them taller, which is easily done. I used parts from several kits to make my bins have the proper height.

The prototype had some distinctive reinforcements consisting of three hoops at the top and vertical bracing going from top to bottom. I made these from various styrene strips. I added brass ladders and scratchbuilt platforms, which also helped make the silos stand out a little more. Finally, the color that you paint the bins also makes them unique.

Evergreen Square Tube 254 (.250") The hatch is made from .020" sheet styrene

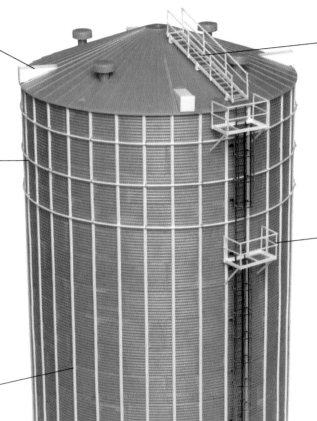

Horizontal reinforcement are made from Evergreen strip styrene 210 (.030" rod) fastened to the silo with U-shaped brackets made of brass wire

Vertical reinforcement is made from Evergreen strip styrene 103 (.010" x .060") and 121 (.020" x .030")

The ladder is from my scrap box. The sides are Evergreen strip styrene 103 (.010" x .060"). Handrails are made from Evergreen strip styrene 120 (.020" x .020") and 100 (.010" x .020").

The platform frame is made from Evergreen strip styrene 291 (.060") angle.
Diagonal supports are Evergreen strip styrene 121 (.020" x .030").
The floor is Scale Scenics SS-3501 Micro Mesh.
The handrail is made from Evergreen strip styrene 120 (.020" x .020") and 100 (.010" x .020").

Walthers Caged Ladders 933-2956

I wanted my bins to have an aged look. New bins are silver, but over the years, the silver look fades and the corrugated metal becomes flat gray with a bluish tint. It took several attempts to match the right color and ended up with a mix made from ModelMaster 1732 Light Gray and 2105 French Dark Blue in the ratio 2:1 which I airbrushed the bins with. My reference photos showed that even older bins didn't look heavily weathered, so I gave mine a subtle weathering. I rubbed the corrugated panels with a stiff brush, some more than others to achieve a slightly less uniform look. Besides rubbing the corrugated panels, I gave the roof a little rust in the form of powdered chalk. The concrete base also received a little brown and gray powdered chalk. The picture at the right shows an unweathered bin next to an weathered bin.

Conveyor

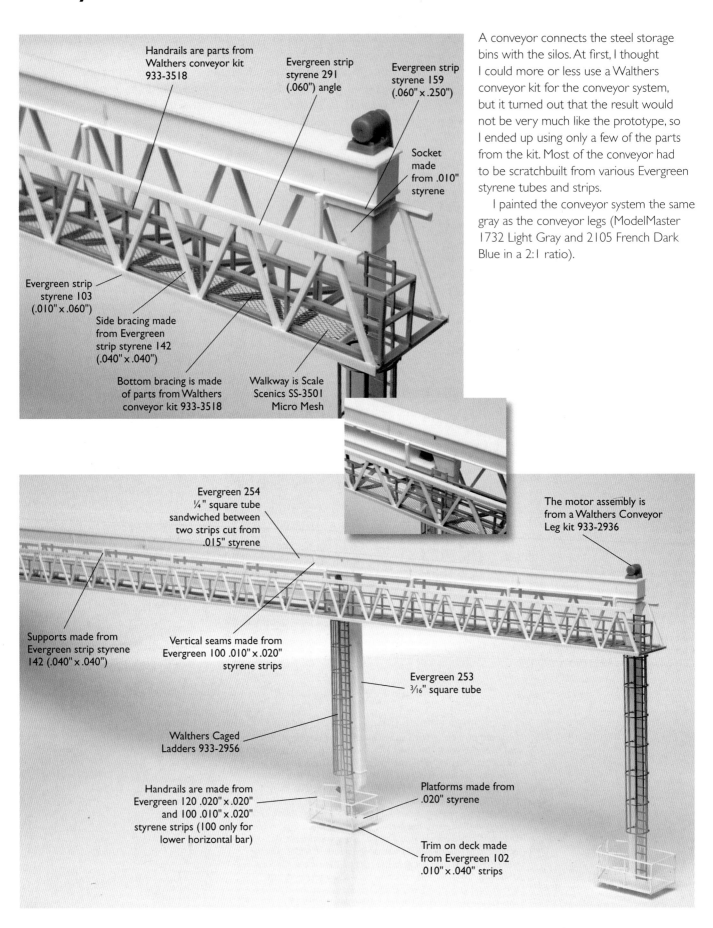

Handrails are parts from Walthers conveyor kit 933-3518

Evergreen strip styrene 291 (.060") angle

Evergreen strip styrene 159 (.060" x .250")

Socket made from .010" styrene

Evergreen strip styrene 103 (.010" x .060")

Side bracing made from Evergreen strip styrene 142 (.040" x .040")

Bottom bracing is made of parts from Walthers conveyor kit 933-3518

Walkway is Scale Scenics SS-3501 Micro Mesh

A conveyor connects the steel storage bins with the silos. At first, I thought I could more or less use a Walthers conveyor kit for the conveyor system, but it turned out that the result would not be very much like the prototype, so I ended up using only a few of the parts from the kit. Most of the conveyor had to be scratchbuilt from various Evergreen styrene tubes and strips.

I painted the conveyor system the same gray as the conveyor legs (ModelMaster 1732 Light Gray and 2105 French Dark Blue in a 2:1 ratio).

Evergreen 254 ¼" square tube sandwiched between two strips cut from .015" styrene

The motor assembly is from a Walthers Conveyor Leg kit 933-2936

Supports made from Evergreen strip styrene 142 (.040" x .040")

Vertical seams made from Evergreen 100 .010" x .020" styrene strips

Evergreen 253 ³⁄₁₆" square tube

Walthers Caged Ladders 933-2956

Handrails are made from Evergreen 120 .020" x .020" and 100 .010" x .020" styrene strips (100 only for lower horizontal bar)

Platforms made from .020" styrene

Trim on deck made from Evergreen 102 .010" x .040" strips

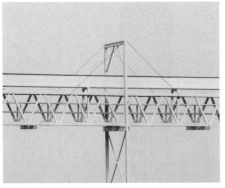

After the parts had been painted and installed, I applied the support wires. I used EZ Line from Berkshire Junction, and elastic string, secured with a tiny dab of CA.

The picture shows the conveyor connecting the bins to the main silos on the prototype.

I made two towers as supports for the conveyor bridge

Evergreen 273 .100" I-beam

Evergreen 252 ⅛" square tube The square tube on the conveyor slips over this

Evergreen 272 .080" I-beam

Cross bracing made from Evergreen strip styrene 141 (.020" x .030")

All horizontal beams except the one at the top are Evergreen 271 .060" I-beams

On a heavy piece of paper, I made a work drawing of the supports.

For the side bracing, I needed a lot of identical pieces of .040" x .040" strip styrene. To make completely uniform diagonal cuts, I taped several .040" x .040" strips next to each other on my cutting mat and made the cuts along a ruler.

Sometimes the strips are not long enough for your needs, and you have to glue two together. When you splice two beams, you get the strongest joint by cutting them diagonally.

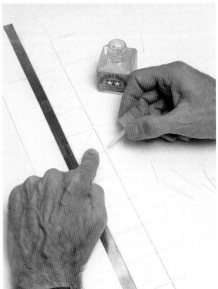

I taped a metal band to the drawing to use as a straightedge for placing the first beam. Then I placed the horizontal beams on the drawing and glued them to the vertical beams one by one.

Truck loading and unloading station

The truck unloading facility on my grain elevator will be almost hidden behind the silos, but I modeled it anyway because you never know if you someday will use the grain facility where it can be viewed from a different angle. I also like knowing that an important element like the truck loading station is there even though you can't see it.

The truck loading and unloading station is one of the structures that had to be built from scratch. I used a variety of Evergreen styrene sheets and strips, Pikestuff panels, and parts from my scrap box to build the structure. The prototype has a double shed, but I only made a single shed for my compressed version of a grain elevator.

The trucks are filled via a discharge pipe coming from the silo and going down through the roof in the shed. The trucks deliver their load through a hole covered with a grill located in the floor.

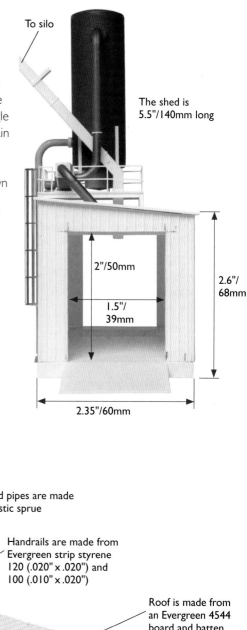

To silo

The shed is 5.5"/140mm long

2"/50mm

1.5"/39mm

2.6"/68mm

2.35"/60mm

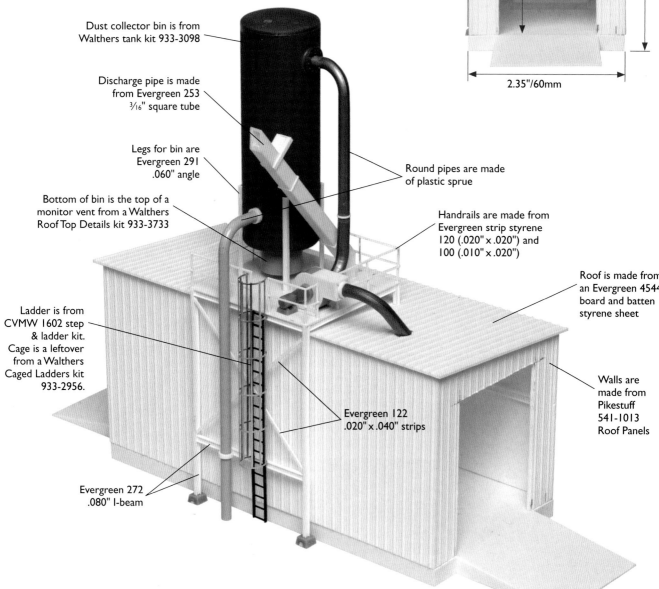

Dust collector bin is from Walthers tank kit 933-3098

Discharge pipe is made from Evergreen 253 ³⁄₁₆" square tube

Legs for bin are Evergreen 291 .060" angle

Bottom of bin is the top of a monitor vent from a Walthers Roof Top Details kit 933-3733

Round pipes are made of plastic sprue

Handrails are made from Evergreen strip styrene 120 (.020" x .020") and 100 (.010" x .020")

Roof is made from an Evergreen 4544 board and batten styrene sheet

Ladder is from CVMW 1602 step & ladder kit. Cage is a leftover from a Walthers Caged Ladders kit 933-2956.

Evergreen 122 .020" x .040" strips

Walls are made from Pikestuff 541-1013 Roof Panels

Evergreen 272 .080" I-beam

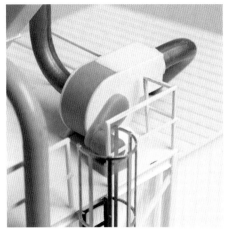

The blower is made from the round top of a monitor vent from a Walthers Roof Top Details kit 933-3733 sandwiched between .020" styrene. The motor assembly is from a Walthers Conveyor Leg kit 933-2936.

This is the truck loading and unloading station on the grain elevator in Lexington, Neb. My version had to be compressed as did the rest of my grain elevator.

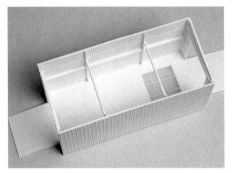

The bracing inside the shed is made from Evergreen 272 .080" I-beams. The grilles in the floor are made from Evergreen strip styrene 120 (.020" x .020").

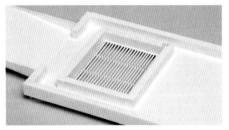

On the floor, seen from below, you can see the edge, which is Evergreen 188 .125" x .188" strips.

I airbrushed the dust collector bin, platform, and other parts gray (ModelMaster 1732 Light Gray and 2105 French Dark Blue in a 2:1 ratio). The floor was airbrushed with a concrete color mixed from ModelMaster 1730 Flat Gull Gray, 1706 Sand, and 1768 Flat White. Unfortunately, I can't give you an exact recipe on the sun-bleached pale pink color I used for the shed. It took many adjustments to my blend to get the right shade. I used light gray, white, beige, and red but lost track of the ratios along the way. The weathering of the shed was done with brown and gray powdered chalk.

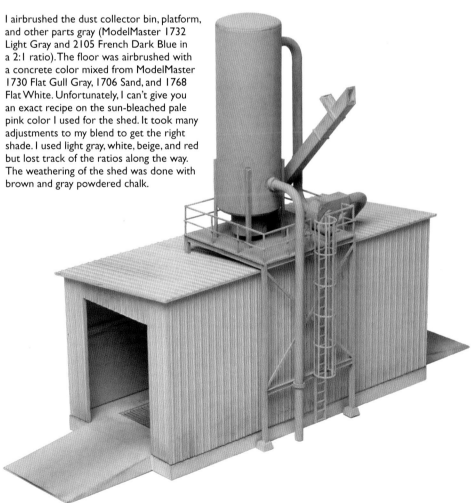

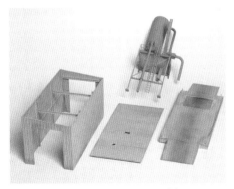

The truck loading station consists of four subassemblies that were painted and weathered before I glued them together permanently.

Modern concrete storage silos

Walthers Corn Storage Silo kit 933-2975 seemed to be a good starting point for these modern concrete storage silos. I also added a few silo sections that were left over from a Walthers coal loader silo kit in my scrap box, which are the gray ones on the first silo.

I scratchbuilt the conveyors that connect the silos to the main silo section, using many of the same materials that I used for the conveyor on the steel bins.

The handrails on top of the silos were made of brass wire instead of styrene strips because they were going to be round. I soldered the parts together first and then bent the handrail in a circle. I drilled holes for the stanchions in the deck and glued the handrail to the silo with cyanoacrylate adhesive.

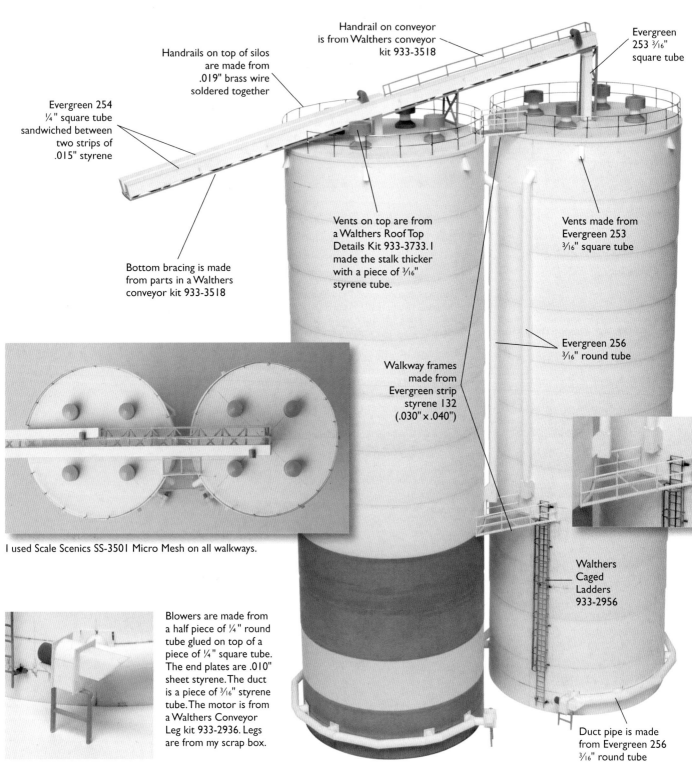

Handrail on conveyor is from Walthers conveyor kit 933-3518

Evergreen 253 ³⁄₁₆" square tube

Handrails on top of silos are made from .019" brass wire soldered together

Evergreen 254 ¼" square tube sandwiched between two strips of .015" styrene

Bottom bracing is made from parts in a Walthers conveyor kit 933-3518

Vents on top are from a Walthers Roof Top Details Kit 933-3733. I made the stalk thicker with a piece of ³⁄₁₆" styrene tube.

Vents made from Evergreen 253 ³⁄₁₆" square tube

Evergreen 256 ³⁄₁₆" round tube

Walkway frames made from Evergreen strip styrene 132 (.030" x .040")

Walthers Caged Ladders 933-2956

I used Scale Scenics SS-3501 Micro Mesh on all walkways.

Blowers are made from a half piece of ¼" round tube glued on top of a piece of ¼" square tube. The end plates are .010" sheet styrene. The duct is a piece of ³⁄₁₆" styrene tube. The motor is from a Walthers Conveyor Leg kit 933-2936. Legs are from my scrap box.

Duct pipe is made from Evergreen 256 ³⁄₁₆" round tube

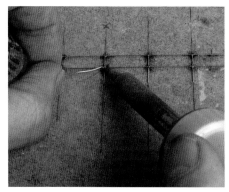

I outlined the handrail on a sheet of MDF board and taped two long pieces of brass wire to it. I then soldered the stanchions to the wires.

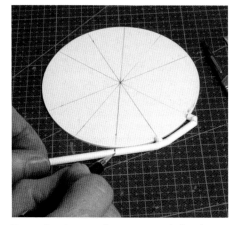

To cut the pieces at the correct angle for the duct pipe, I made a template.

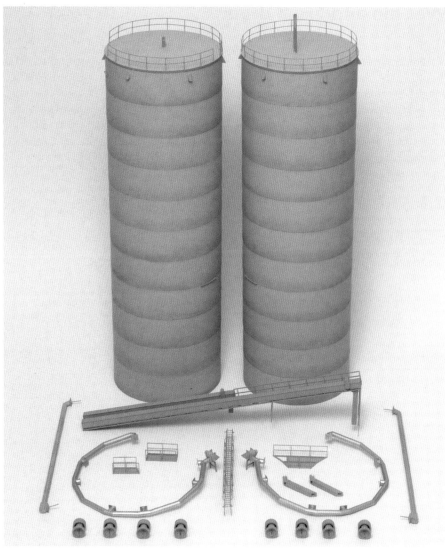

All parts, except for the top handrails, could be taken off the silo and be painted separately. The conveyor, pipes, and vents received the same gray color as the similar parts on the other sections.

I first sprayed the silos with a base coat of Tamiya AS-2 Light Gray. Even though Tamiya calls it light gray, it is more medium gray than light gray.

I then dabbed the silos with ModelMaster 1732 Light Gray. I chose cooler gray shades for these silos because new concrete is more of a cool gray than old concrete is.

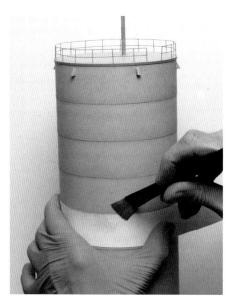

To enhance the banding effect, I wrapped a piece of paper around the silo and applied some gray powdered chalk along the edge using upward brush strokes.

Wet bin and grain dryer

Most of the grain elevators I saw on my trip to the Midwest, including the one in Lexington, Neb., had grain dryers that were shaped like towers. To my knowledge, no manufacturer offers such a grain dryer as a kit. The only grain dryer you can get as a kit is the old style dryer offered by Walthers. I would have preferred to have a tower-style grain dryer, but I estimated that it would be to much work to build one from scratch. Instead, I bought the Walthers grain dryer kit and a Walthers wet bin kit for my grain facility. If someone later comes out with a grain dryer tower, I can always replace those pieces.

I connected the bins to the conveyor leg with pipes that came with the conveyor leg kit.

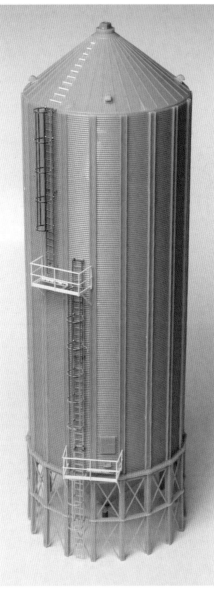

A Walthers grain dryer (933-3124) and surge bin (933-2935) represents the grain-drying part of my grain elevator. I only made a few modifications to the kits. I applied brass ladders and scratchbuilt platforms so they would match the look of the platforms on the rest of the grain facility. I chipped away the molded steps on the roof and replaced them with new ones made from .020" x .020" styrene strip.

The wet bin is a Walthers wet/dry grain bin kit (933-2937). I didn't use the platforms and ladders that came with the kit. Instead, I used caged brass ladders from Gold Medal Models (87-12). I made the platforms as I did on the rest of the grain facility. The molded steps on the roof were replaced with new ones made from styrene strip similar to those on the surge bin.

I airbrushed the two bins a cool light gray color mixed from Model Master 1728 Light Ghost Gray, 1733 Camouflage Gray, and 1768 Flat White in a 1:1:1 ratio. The grain dryer received the same gray as the conveyors on top of the silos (ModelMaster 1732 Light Gray and 2105 French Dark Blue in a 2:1 ratio). I applied scattered rust spots using dry powdered chalk.

Concrete floor

I prefer using plaster when making paved and concrete areas. I have tried using styrene sheets for streets but it doesn't work for me. Even after the styrene has been painted and weathered, the surface still doesn't have a concrete or asphalt feel to it. Plaster has a slightly non-uniform surface, which, to me, looks very realistic.

I use Woodland Scenics Smooth-It plaster. It is easy to work with and easy to sand as well. I painted the plastered area with a light concrete color mixed from Humbrol 147 Light Gray, 34 White, and 121 Pale Stone in a 2:2:1 ratio. I thinned the paint so it ends up almost like a wash and applied it in three or four layers. I let each layer dry completely before I applied the next layer. The first layer acts as a primer and seals the surface. Finally, I gave the surface a dark wash (a few drops of Vallejo Air 71052 German Gray mixed with water and a little rubbing alcohol).

Like the grain facility in Lexington, Neb., my grain elevator also has a concrete floor at the filling area.

1. I made a frame from two styrene strips placed along the inside of the rails and attached to a square piece of styrene sheet in each end. I also used styrene to make a spatula with a recessed edge.

2. I outlined the area on each side of the track with foam tape. I then filled the areas including the one between the rails with Woodland Scenics Smooth-It.

3. I smoothed the plaster with the spatula. The recessed edge on the spatula ensures that the top of plaster layer will be a little below the top edge of the rail.

4. After the plaster had dried, I carefully removed the styrene frame and the masking tape.

5. I placed the silos against the plastered area and filled the gaps with plaster. I dripped water on the dry plaster before I applied the new plaster.

6. I let the plaster dry for several days before I sanded the surface smooth. I used a piece of sandpaper glued to a piece of a wood as a sanding stick.

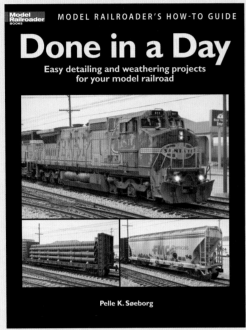
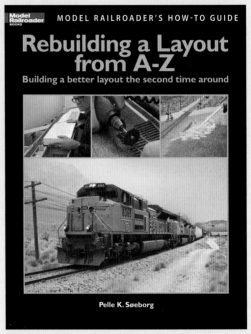